My Life as a Boy

My Life as a Boy

KIM CHERNIN

ALGONQUIN BOOKS OF CHAPEL HILL 1997

Published by
ALGONQUIN BOOKS OF CHAPEL HILL
Post Office Box 2225
Chapel Hill, North Carolina 27515-2225

a division of
WORKMAN PUBLISHING
708 Broadway
New York, New York 10003

Library of Congress Cataloging-in-Publication Data
Chernin, Kim.
    My life as a boy : a woman's story / Kim Chernin.
      p.   cm.
    ISBN 1-56512-163-5
    1. Chernin, Kim—Biography.   2. Women authors,
   American—20th century—Biography.   3. Lesbians—
   United States—Biography.   I. Title.
   PS3553.H3558Z468   1997
   813'.54—dc21
   [b]   96-53978
                                    CIP

10 9 8 7 6 5 4 3 2 1
First Edition

For Renate

Part 1

1

No one who knew me back then thought I would turn into a boy. I looked the way many women do in their thirties, ample and proud of it. In our family pictures there is Max with his long hair, our small daughter Larissa in tie-dyed shirts and jeans. I am usually wearing low-cut long dresses. We seem to be on our way to a costume party, but that's the way a lot of people looked, especially in Berkeley, during the seventies: the men with beards, the women in fringed shawls and ethnic blouses. No, I never expected to turn into a boy. But that is a dangerous time in the life of a woman, when she is still in her thirties and her only daughter is off to college.

Yes, a dangerous time. It involves a break with the past, the anticipation of a sudden freedom, no kids in the house, a new beginning for the mother, as if she too and not only the daughter were taking off into her own life. Anything possible. Future unknown. Time for the unlived life to rise up and stake its claim. Everything you might have been but didn't become; anything you might have wished to be but put aside. Now's your chance.

Some people won't let anything happen to them until they can explain how it could happen; therefore nothing much happens and they spend their time fending off the unlikely. I didn't want that to happen to me. I didn't want to stay as I was, hidden away in my own private world, in my second marriage, because there was no reason, none that anyone else would find convincing, to leave.

If a woman in her thirties turns into a boy, that may mean she's having trouble getting out of the place she's in. She requires the instinctive, wholly natural ruthlessness of a boy. He will leave home; everyone expects it of him. He won't move in next door to his mother or around the block and raise children, not likely. He won't give it a second thought: he's off into the world, he's a boy, he's going.

I've watched boys take off. I've seen them on bikes, skateboards, motor scooters, sliding on a piece of waxed cardboard. They fly down the middle of the street, cars going fast uphill, downhill, do they care? The direction of a boy is straight out the door, down the hill, out of the neighborhood, into the world. No second thought at leaving people behind, leaving them to fend for themselves as he takes off, hellbent for his own future without them.

I've seen girls on skateboards and girls on waxed cardboard, but I never saw a girl who did not look back and wonder. Not ever. Because there is always someone standing at the door, someone waiting for you to come home, someone who will be happier when they hear your key in the lock. Girls are always aware of this and boys are not.

Women, especially mothers, know in every moment who is waiting for them to get back home, to call in, to fetch them; this knowledge is what it means to be a woman. Therefore the fate of a girl, the future she's definitely growing into, holds the certainty of restriction. But for a boy, as I have often observed, there is little danger of becoming a woman. He can be as reckless, as ruthless as he pleases, as carefree, devil-may-care as he likes, breaking his mother's heart, casting off the girl who's waiting for him in the garden. This guy has got to go to sea, and so he's off.

If ever the boy stops being a boy (and this is not inevitable), the man he becomes will have no more impulse, in being a man, to fret over the people he's left behind. This ease is never possible for the girl. Even if she went from girl to woman in her father's house, she'd be thinking about the people downstairs, for whom she is not baking while she is writing poetry. A real artist, they say, goes on perpetrating whatever creative act he's involved in, even if the children are crying; he doesn't stop, he doesn't look up, he doesn't even bat an eyelash. According to this, no woman is ever an artist.

Of course, these days girls are almost everything boys are. But if you are a woman at that dangerous time in your life, when you have just lost a reason for going on being the way you've been, if your kids have gone from home, or someone ill or aging you've been caring for has just died, it won't do you much good to turn into a girl, not even a tough girl who can kick a ball, who knows how to fight when a good fight is needed, can curse, will race her brothers and sometimes beat them. It won't do much good because this tough girl must not cry. If she ever wants to get away from home, to leave, to have a future of her own, she has to sacrifice the soft and sensitive romantic yearnings the boy can keep for a time, can even use, to get him out into the world.

There he is, standing in the rain outside his girl's window. To-morrow he will spot a woman on the bus and take off, passion-ately, desperately, into the world to follow her. The tough girl cannot allow herself so much need for another person. The boy weeps when his girl lets him down, walks through the park all night in his bare feet, renews his love by plunging himself into an ice-cold baptismal woodland pool. He is young but he will love her forever. The tough girl has got to prove that she needs no one.

The tough girl, under this pressure, may come to have more in common with a hard man than she has with a boy. In the girl and in the man, something infinitely tender has had to be crushed to achieve a semblance of autonomy. The boy has not yet had to make this sacrifice. For a brief, endangered season of grace, he remains a creature of accomplished paradox, holding simultane-ously the capacity for profound attachment and the ability to break it off, when he must, to follow his own course.

2

When Max and I bought our house in the early seventies, there were no windows opening out onto the vast inland sea first "discovered" in 1769 by Sergeant Ortega, of the Portola exploring party. He and his men, hunting for deer, climbed the eastern grassy slopes of the East Bay and beheld a view similar to the one still visible today when the fog is up.

Still visible today? Well, that's what I used to say, standing on the deck, when we first bought the house. My mother and my husband didn't know whether to take me seriously, but my daughter knew that I was serious. Of course, taking an idea seriously is not quite the same as taking it literally, a distinction my mother could never make.

In those days, whenever my mother visited, we used to walk down to the Euclid Avenue Rose Garden. My mother cherished it, not primarily for its fifty varieties of roses, but even more because it was one of the WPA projects that, at the instigation of the radical movement, had put unemployed men back to work during the thirties.

The past I cherished was more remote. I claimed to behold the long-forgotten sloughs and channels, the dark marshes, the oak savannas, the streams winding through cottonwoods to fall hard down into the plains, which had been the Berkeley landscape before European settlers arrived to change it all. I told my mother that I could, in the haze of an early dawn, make out the smoke rising from the Huchiun villages along the shore of the San Francisco Bay, where the freeway runs now.

It was odd that I said these things to my mother, the last person in the world who could have made sense of them. She gave me that narrow-eyed look she had turned on me since I was a child, then shook her head and probably concluded that youth must be allowed a certain extravagance, a sentiment with which I concur. Why else would we tell the stories of our younger days?

The house where I have lived for twenty-three years is a survivor. It was built just before the fire of 1923, when much of Berkeley burned down, so that Maybeck, our most celebrated local architect, then refused to build in wood and designed instead in Spanish stucco, a fine example of which can be seen right down the street from my house.

These days I cultivate a more precise sense of the particular: the cracked foundation of my house, the continual conversation with my neighbor about the collapsing fence, a hesitant, somewhat guilty love for the steep hill neighborhood, its whimsical, romantic wildness, firs and pines eight stories high, wide streets lined with sycamores, early blossoming cherry and plum trees, already in flower when an occasional late snow falls in March. A neighborhood of pointed, gabled roofs, half-timbered houses, Spanish balconies, overgrown gardens, old roses, winding streets, parks, walks, lanes, alleys, steep stairways, hanging all too splendidly, I often think, in a lofty, elite indifference above the grim neighborhoods along the bay, most of them barely visible from my house, which has long since acquired windows facing the bay. We look westward, with a majestic sweep north and south across the three arched bridges of the bay, unless your eye falls into the flatlands, to the working-class neighborhood where industrial plants, warehouses, retail business, and tough, decaying streets still occasionally house the descendants of the Irish, French, Chinese, Finn, and German workers who settled the area during the 1850s, although the neighborhoods are now substantially African-American and Hispanic. There, the work of reclaiming old Victorian buildings has recently begun, adding significant numbers of old residents to Berkeley's two thousand homeless people, many of whom can be found by day or night in People's Park, a center of radical struggles during the sixties.

Some years ago there were protests in my neighborhood for many weeks about the cutting down of a majestic oak tree in the courtyard of the theological seminary, where new buildings were going up. Even I, who kept to myself in those days, felt compelled to join the crowd that formed illegally. Many of us, perfect strangers to one another, embraced, linked arms, stood silently holding hands as the great tree was dismembered. Late in the afternoon, I found myself standing next to a woman who had put her head on my shoulder and was crying silently. I took off my jacket; I put it around her shoulders. I was taller than she was, the sort of person someone would lean up against, the strong one, the one who can support the other.

That was, I suppose, the day I first began to be a boy.

I don't want to make a big deal of this because it never seemed strange or unnatural to me. People accept many things as fixed and immutable that are in fact subject to change. It had been a cold afternoon, with a tart, forbidding feel to it; we had huddled together against the gusts of early autumn wind. The woman leaning against me, the metallic whine of the chain saw, the smell of raw wood and sawdust. If I were a boy, I thought, if I were standing here with my arm around this woman, I would not let her go until the warm, sweet-earth strength of her was taken in. If I were a boy, I told myself, she would not hand me back my jacket without a promise of meeting up with me again tonight or tomorrow. Right then, out of my hopeless yearning and desire, something seemed to shift and crystallize inside me. My mournful passivity fell away as if I had been subject to a transformation as violent as the tree's fall. It was as if the vital force of the great tree had been transferred to me because a woman had cried for it while I held her in my arms. Many years later I would again meet up with this woman, Alix Graham, and learn a lot from her.

So, I was becoming a boy. I could see that this might have serious consequences. My husband, although certainly a generous and liberal man, might prefer to have me dreamy and dependent, as I had been for many years. A change of this sort would probably also be disturbing to my daughter. A mother who turned into a boy? My daughter would probably resent this. And I myself? Was I ready to emerge from my dreamy life?

Boys are restless and they are always up to mischief. I had a daily quarrel in fourth grade with the boy who sat behind me, who liked to tug at my pigtails and poke me. It was hard to imagine a boy living the life I lived. Meditating, writing down his dreams, reading books on alchemy, writing love poems to god. There were nice boys, who walked you home from school because they felt you needed their protection. There were naughty boys, who stole bottles from the supermarket and sold them back to the liquor store. A boy acted before he thought, punched people out when they gave him trouble, devoted his life to not being a girl. A boy had certain rights that came from being a boy and were born along with him. These included a right to want, to take, to desire, to possess, to conquer, a right to the body's pleasures, a right to women.

I had already learned that you can't tamper with a transformational imperative. But all things considered, I thought it might be a good idea to observe the process of becoming a boy, to try gently, where possible, to slow it down. Young people have a tragic sense of life. It's not their fault, nature has designed it that way. Only very young people have what it takes to survive youth. No one else could put up with the high excitements, the violent endings, the stormy beginnings. I gather young people are not like that anymore. Perhaps youth got to be too much even for the young? But that's how we were in my day.

My daughter left for college. Sometime later, I knew that I wanted to leave my marriage. I was restless. I seemed to be waiting for some crucial event that would announce the call to adventure. It would have something to do with falling in love. Love was, for most of us back then, the most easily recognized form of transformation. I knew about love, but I never imagined the change it had in store for me. I knew about women, too, but I never imagined a woman like this one.

3

I will call her Hadamar, after the small town in central Germany where her family had their country house. A Jewish family of that thoroughly assimilated kind that has never seemed very Jewish to me (probably because my family comes from Eastern Europe), they had arrived in America during the thirties, thanks to the foresight, or even prescience, of her father's eldest sister, who had urged the entire family—aunts, uncles, nephews and nieces, even the ailing grandmother—to liquidate house, land, holdings and emigrate while there was still time. On the mother's side, Hadamar was connected to a large banking family from southern Italy, people with an international culture, considerable wealth, and family connections in most of the world's great cities. They were all fluent in several languages, held high posts in banking and commercial enterprises, would support, sponsor, educate, and, when necessary, marry off their poorer relations with the help of substantial dowries.

When I met Hadamar, who had been a very small child during the family's migration from Europe, she was living not far from me on a hill street in North Berkeley. Several cousins and their families, and an aging sister of her father, lived close by in the same neighborhood, where their entire branch of the family had settled after a brief time in New York. They had spent a year or two in England, where her father had not felt secure. He was a successful industrialist, son of a self-made man of enormous energy, unflagging will, and great family feeling, all of which had been passed down to him, the eldest son. Hadamar scarcely remembered their migration, although she knew the name of the small town in the Cotswolds where she had celebrated her fourth birthday. Her family called her Hadi, a name she had used more or less officially since she began school, but I always called her Hadamar, even before I fell in love with her.

We met at the home of Edith Bonheim, her father's older sister, who, for several weeks, had been telling me stories about her childhood. While I was saying good-bye to the old woman, hesitating whether to shake hands or embrace, because the conversation, in German, had gone well and we had grown fond of each other, there was a great bustle on the stairs. The door flew open, two small girls in shorts scampered in, followed by a golden retriever and a slender, dark-haired woman who looked at me with surprise, perhaps because she did not expect her aunt to have visitors so late in the day.

I, too, looked at her with surprise. She seemed to carry herself in perpetual motion even when she was standing perfectly still. She had a vibrant shimmer that reminded me of a hummingbird. I knew that I could not trust my first impressions. I thought she was tall but later found out she was no taller than I was. I saw her through a luminous haze, as if she were standing far away down a long, hot road and heat waves were rising from her.

The old woman drew her close, murmuring, *"Hadamar, liebe Hadamar,"* which made the girls whoop and scamper about shouting, "Ha-da-mar, Ha-da-mar, Ha-da-mar," while she and I said hello to each other.

She laughed, with a nod at the girls. "I am called Hadi," she explained to me, while glancing affectionately at the old woman, who had taken her niece's hand between both her own and was now shaking her head in a way I have seen old people do, who have had to get used to strange ways and have done so graciously, but not without some inner protest.

"Hadamar," the old woman repeated. She was about to say more, I thought, then reminded herself she had probably said it before and so changed her mind and fell silent.

The younger woman was gazing attentively at me. "You are the woman doing the oral histories?" she suggested tentatively, perhaps because she preferred to figure it out herself rather than ask directly.

When I nodded she raised her eyebrows with an expression I thought might have been a shade self-satisfied. She seemed more interested in having guessed correctly than in me. What a haughty, superior look she showed in that moment, the first in which I saw her clearly. I was struck by the cool appraisal in her dark eyes, as if she were trying to determine whether I deserved my small, local reputation. She stood very erect, her head high, her pale face with its chiseled features softened by a mass of waving brown hair. I had caught a glimpse of a hidden, hereditary pride, which was then quickly stowed away behind her wonderful social ease.

"Aunt Edith has been longing for us to meet," she acknowledged with a wry smile. "She is convinced we must become friends. I've known her all my life and she's never wrong." She paused to let her words fulfill their playfulness. Then, gaily, with a light shake of her head, "Are you prepared for the dreadful weight of a new friendship?"

I thought Hadamar might have said more than she intended to say; perhaps she imagined her stilted speech and grand manner were an adequate disguise for anything serious. She now seemed to be looking at me as if she wanted me to guess something. People were always telling me I made too much of things. I imagined that might have been happening then, too. She flushed slightly; her dark eyes took on, I thought, a secretive, searching look. Now, all at once, I recognized her. This was the woman I had been preparing to meet for a long time, had been dreaming up and waiting for and had now found.

Then, for an instant or two — I believe it could not have been much more—everything grew quiet. The dog had come over to lie down at the old woman's feet, his grave, golden head resting familiarly against her toes. The girls had plopped down on the floor next to him and were looking up at Hadamar, whom I already knew I would call by no other name, perhaps from a feeling for what is old and has vanished, a nostalgia I must have shared with the old woman. She, who had by now taken me by the hand, so that she was holding Hadamar with one hand, me by the other, nodded her head absently, far removed from us, while this dark-eyed woman and I, who had met only moments before, were left standing face to face, silently, expectantly, at the beginning of a friendship that would find us, when it ended, different from what we had been before we met. The ending of it seemed as clearly stated as its moody, contradictory beginning, so that the friendship with Hadamar began, at least for me, with an immediate sense of inexplicable sorrow. I felt that I had lost her even before I had told her my name.

There are women who have to be courted out of an imperious sense that wanting them is reason enough to have them. I myself had once been a woman like that. Could I possibly have known, in that dense, brief silence, that to have this woman I would have to change beyond recognition?

Aunt Edith, rousing herself from her thoughts, aware perhaps of an awkwardness or disharmony for which she was responsible, introduced me solemnly to Hadamar. "Kim, our dear Kim," she said in that oddly inflected English of educated foreigners who will never really be at home here. "This is the woman who has stepped into our life and just like that she has opened wide the doors of memory."

Our dear Kim, whose last name must have been unnecessary, because we had already embraced her as one of our own? Hadamar seemed to take it in that sense. She now smiled warmly as the old woman brought our hands together. I noticed that Hadamar was close to my age, probably in her late thirties. Her smile, the silence through which we had just passed, had made a bond between us; there was no mistaking it. Things happen like that between women, although usually not much attention is paid to silences; they slip by and nothing much comes of them.

4

For many years before my daughter left for college, I always roused myself in the late afternoons when she came home from school. She has since told me how little I succeeded in my pretense that I shared a world with her. I was remote, faraway, dreamy, lost in myself, never quite accessible, although she had sympathy for how hard I tried and so she tried herself not to feel lonely. In this shared effort to be what we were not, we both failed.

This dreaminess was my private life, set apart from marriage and social arrangements, and for a time it seemed that Hadamar would belong to the social world that never touched the life I lived within myself. Women are often like this; many hide it better than I did.

The two little girls who showed up with Hadamar the day we first met were not her children but distant cousins or grandnieces. There were always so many people around Hadamar, coming and going, spending the night, stopping in to stay for a time between jobs or love affairs. I never figured out the exact relationships between Hadamar and her entourage. Her extended family was so large it was hard to keep track of them, people arriving from Europe or South America, all with a claim to hospitality in the beautiful house that had belonged to her parents. Even the golden retriever wasn't her dog.

She wasn't living with her husband, she wasn't quite divorced, she certainly wasn't lonely. She was one of those very attractive women who find it easy to get people to fall in love with them, who run themselves ragged trying to maintain all the relationships that promise love. I don't think she'd ever really had a friend before.

The quiet that had been there when Hadamar and I met, the kind of silence in which whatever happens, happens significantly, that is the sort of event dreamy people hold on to. They remember it, it sinks into them, they always later say it has changed them. Sometimes they say it has changed them forever. But for more worldly people the impressions of such things are usually so slight they are remembered, when you remind them, only with difficulty, and then only because it is flattering to them, because they have made so deep an impression on you. But at the time I had no idea there was this sort of difference between Hadamar and me. I used to assume, if I felt something strongly, the other person did, too, and that, I suppose, is a kind of innocence.

Hadamar had founded an arts organization in the East Bay.

She knew everyone who painted, danced, composed, sang, sculpted, wove, stitched, wrote plays. She could, at a moment's notice, organize an exhibit, an outdoor festival, a trek through open studios, making connections, introducing potential collaborators. With her vivacity, tireless energy, that radiant smile of hers, the infectious laughter, she could always get people to donate their time. Over the years she had raised quite a lot of money for charity.

She could have been anything, that was the impression she gave me. When she was younger she had sculpted and painted. She had a deep, beautiful, perhaps contralto voice I heard once, when we were out walking in the woods. I always wanted to hear it again, but she had given up singing and only sang when she had forgotten someone else was there, or didn't know that she was singing.

Sometimes when I was with her I felt that I was lying in wait, that if I was still enough, scarcely breathing, for long enough, she would suddenly reveal whatever was hidden behind her elaborately cultivated artifice. She reminded me then of a young doe when it comes out of the woods and encounters us, those ominous, awkward two-legged creatures, for the first time. But I don't think anyone else ever saw Hadamar in this way.

I ran into her the second time at her aunt's house. I was leaving, she was coming up the stairs with the golden retriever and one of the little girls I had met before. The dog and the child seemed to recognize me, but I had the impression Hadamar did not quite recall who I was. Or was she pretending? Some people, when you make an impression on them, for whatever reason, will try to act nonchalant the next time you meet, as if they haven't given you a thought meanwhile. But I had been thinking about Hadamar. Was she the woman for whom I would change my life? Who would she have to be to be that one? I had come by to visit her aunt at the same time on the same day of the week, one week later, and I never thought it was a coincidence that Hadamar showed up then, too.

I reminded her who I was.

She laughed, repeating what I had said.

"The woman doing the oral histories, of course, yes, I hadn't forgotten. I asked my aunt about you. Did she tell you about the book fair? Will you read?"

The golden retriever had run off down the street. The little girl was bumping down the steps on her bottom, kicking up her legs and shrieking with pleasure.

"Hush, Deena, I can't hear myself think." Hadamar reproached her gently, but it was clear the child would pay her no mind. A few minutes later the little girl ran off after the golden retriever; she was soon pulling up grass in a neighbor's yard.

"I don't much read in public. If I did I would certainly partic-ipate. But no, I told Edith, I would have to refuse."

I wondered, while we were talking, if the stillness would come again. I kept waiting for some sign that our first meeting had been significant for her, too. If she was the woman I was looking for, wouldn't she, too, be looking for me?

"You don't read in public?" She seemed surprised, then looked at me suspiciously. "But aren't you a writer? My aunt said . . ."

"A writer who is not yet ready to publish."

She frowned, disappointed I thought. And so I added, quickly, "Although I have had opportunities."

"But the oral histories? Surely you are planning to publish them?"

I had no idea what I was planning to do with the oral histories. I liked old people, especially those who had come from distant places. I knew they liked telling stories and appreciated a good listener. Some of them looked forward to seeing the stories written down, but most of them just wanted someone to listen. That suited me, because I liked spending time with them, especially in the afternoon when my own work was finished for the day. They were so glad to see me, they never asked questions, I felt at ease with them because they never expected me to talk about myself. I drank tea with them, they brought out a special box of chocolate or homemade cookies, and some of them told me the same story every time I came. I was always interested in the occasional changes that showed up, although sometimes it was only a change of inflection or a hesitation that had not been there before.

Hadamar was still frowning. She was, I could tell, used to sizing people up quickly. Perhaps she thought I was being coy or disingenuous or had presented myself to her aunt falsely as someone gathering stories for a book about Jewish life in Germany before the war.

"Sometimes one writes because the writing is an end in itself, a meditation, even at times a kind of descent," I said, although I felt there was not much point in saying it. The woman I was trying to find would not have needed so much explanation. "And that's the same reason I listen to stories."

"You're quite serious? You write without intending to publish? You are collecting stories but have no idea what you will do with them?"

"Well, I have sometimes thought the stories would figure it out. When they figure it out I'm sure they'll let me know and then I'll do it, whatever it is."

"Oh, I see," she said slowly and, I thought, derisively.

But then suddenly she seemed to decide that I was joking. She tossed her head, throwing her hair back over her shoulders, and that was the first time I heard her famous laugh and yes, believe me, it was beautiful, a low, deep, appreciative chuckle that brought a look of searching, playful complicity into her eyes, as if we had just become conspirators.

"I won't ask again." She raised her hands as if to promise. "Writers have their secrets."

"Oh no," I answered, still not quite certain why she had laughed. "It's not we who have the secrets. No, not at all. It's the secrets that have us."

5

My friend Lillian, who has known me all these years, says that I gave the impression back then of someone who had been living in a cave. Years before, I had been reasonably sociable, outgoing; I traveled around by myself and made friends easily. Now that I was coming out of my cave, the world looked strange to me. I had to study everything I came across. Suddenly a tree would rise up at the edge of the woods and strike me forcefully with its presence. Ah, I would say to myself, so this is a tree, and a kind of perilous wonder would descend on me as if I had never before beheld a tree.

I live in this house, I used to say to myself with a feeling of discovery, although I had been living in the house for a good seven years. That tall young man coming down the street is our neighbor's son, I would inform myself, although I must have seen him on his way to school or work practically every day.

When I would explain this condition to Max, my husband, he would put aside whatever he was doing, lean back in his chair, and listen to me. Sometimes I would talk for hours, while he smoked or sipped a cup of cold coffee, really listening, devotedly listening to me, although I'm not sure what he could make of it. Make of it? What could he make of it?

When you live in a cave you're not exactly asleep even if it seems to the rest of the world that you're dreaming. A cave dweller of the type I mean, living a step or two removed from the world, venturing out under carefully regulated conditions, may have an intensely active inner life of which she rarely speaks.

Most people don't know that you can be perfectly awake, aware of everything going on around you, as fully awake as anyone who is driving a car or stirring eggs for breakfast, yet at the same time be concentrating on something else, as if you are being called, or spoken to, as if you are being seriously addressed and it would be a good thing if you listened.

It's not a question of hearing voices or going crazy—no, absolutely nothing like that. There are worlds, experiences, dimensions; how is one to talk about them? If I could have told Max about them, if they were tellable between a woman and a man, I would never have left him, I wouldn't have gone out looking for people who knew what I meant and were already living in the way I wanted to be living. Later on, after our marriage had broken up, I found these women living right in our neighborhood, doing things I had imagined but never really believed women could be doing together, and I don't just mean sex, although sex is part of it.

I said to Max, the first time I tried to tell him about the cave life I lived (my real life I might have said, but that would have hurt him): "It's like this . . ."

But then I couldn't go on.

"I'm listening," he said, and that was the right thing to say.

"This world, right here, in the room, in our house, outside in the garden . . . it seems so real to people, this is what is meant by the real world, how we are together, our life with Larissa, this is reality. But for me, no, there's another reality, and sometimes I think it's even more real, or perhaps not more real, but strangely vivid, intensely alive in a way that our shared world, our common, consensual world, is not."

I thought he was sifting through my words, trying to find something in them that was like his own experience. He looked grave—not exactly worried, puzzled perhaps.

"I've had the impression you were much happier lately. You've seemed more at ease, as if you were coming out of yourself. I thought you were much less depressed."

"Depressed? Not depressed? But these words only have meaning where we live, together. Not that I'm depressed *because* I'm with you. If I'm depressed *when* I'm with you it's because I've come out of another way of being with myself. And then I miss it. I miss myself. It's as if I have lost myself in coming back to you, as if I undergo a narrowing of some kind, a loss of potential. Not that it's your fault. Of course it's not your fault. But between us, well, you occupy the position of the man. So then, I'm the woman. It seems perfectly natural, but what if it isn't? What if it were more natural for me to be more like the man sometimes, while you were more like the woman? I'm sorry. It's hard to explain. I'm just trying to say there's some way we have of being together in which I can't be all of what I am when I'm by myself, which is when I can be more of myself. You see?"

I could tell he was trying not to be hurt. If he was hurt and showed it, I would feel misunderstood and get angry and grow silent.

But how could he not be hurt? I was saying that the only real life I knew was when I was not with him.

"When I come home early you always seem pleased to see me," he said very quietly, but I could tell how sad he was.

I ran over and threw my arms around his neck. I got into his lap, snuggling down small, willing to disappear in the comfort any touch of his brought. If I was crying, they were probably his tears.

He covered my head with kisses. "You're safe," he said, and I felt safe. "We'll work it out," he whispered, but I no longer believed him.

The time had come, this is what I was trying to tell him. My life as a man's woman had come to an end. It was time to care more for my own desires than for any other obligation. My time had come to take on the world like a boy.

During the last year of our marriage, we both got the impression we weren't going to be together for long, although neither of us mentioned it to the other. This knowledge was there as we were waking or sleeping, a strange third presence that had entered between us unbidden. Sometimes, when I woke up at night, I would find him awake, leaning on his elbow, gazing at me.

"We have to do something," I would say. "If we go on like this we won't go on for long."

"Yes," he would sigh, putting his arms around me, resigned, fatalistic, as we both silently told ourselves there were things we could do.

Maybe at that time in his life he didn't want a relationship with a woman who was awake. Some men are like that, they fall in love with the dreaminess of the woman. When we first met he used to dream he was running or riding fast and was coming to save me. Once, when he dreamed I was fatally wounded, he woke up crying. I had never been loved the way this man loved me, but perhaps he could not love a woman who was awake or who no longer needed saving.

One day I saw him getting out of the car, wearing his heavy hiking boots, just as tall and slim as he'd always been. It was as if I had never seen him before. He was like the tree, the boy next door, the very house itself in which we lived, so familiar I no longer knew them, and now suddenly there he was, happy to see me, with the kind of face you're pleased to see on a man you call your husband.

You'll never find a better one, I said to myself.

Was I looking for a better one?

"It's over, it's all over," I said to him when he came close enough to put my arms around him.

He comforted me, the way he always did. He couldn't know there was no comfort, not for him, not for me, for what was coming between us, even if I brought it about because I wanted it.

I loved to be wrapped up in his arms. I loved to wear his father's suede jacket. I loved it when two of my hands could fit in one of his. I loved the way he loved my daughter. We used to say he had probably saved her childhood for her. We used to say he had certainly saved my life.

6

A woman could, of course, become a boy anywhere in the world, but a place like Berkeley makes the transition seem a good deal more likely. There are people in this town who believe that anything that takes place anywhere in the world, anything new and enterprising and radical and visionary, will happen first in Berkeley. For an outsider, overhearing these things in casual conversation, it would be difficult to say whether they were meant literally, or in the larger spirit of metaphor.

I have always been drawn to the idea of Berkeley as a microcosm, an exemplary little world in which all of the larger world can be found, if only you look hard enough. Aunt Edith's friends, who told me their life stories, were a good example of this. They were a rootless society of the kind Berkeley could very well accommodate, closing it up in itself on obscure hill streets from which you could only retrace your steps, half wondering as you went down if you would ever make your way back up. Hadamar and her friends, even Aunt Edith, who was so solid a presence, gave me the impression they could, at any moment, fade back into their obscure European past, as if they were something I myself had conjured up, ghosts, fantasy companions created for a wet winter day by a lonely child.

I used to transcribe their tapes myself, because I loved to listen to the sound of memory returning, a suspension in breath, the inflection that fell unexpectedly on particular words as events long forgotten made their way back. I, who never felt at home anywhere, was at home in that little bit of once-assimilated Jewish Europe, a world eliminated from history except for small survivor colonies that had sought refuge in places like Berkeley—where, in spite of our perennial housing shortage, there is always room for the past.

Max came with me occasionally, because he was happy about this project that had finally drawn me out of myself and because he, too, was a good listener. In this way a small social world was created through Aunt Edith. The circle grew over time, with invitations to anniversaries and birthday parties and then more intimate family occasions. When Larissa came home from college during one summer vacation we were invited for dinner by the grandniece of Edgar Rosenwasser, my friend who had played chess with Trotsky. He had once described having lunch with Trotsky's wife and boys at their winter villa in Huetteldorf. They wore their coats indoors, he told me, because the place was not winterized. It was at the home of Edgar Rosenwasser's grandniece that I ran into Hadamar for the third time, unexpectedly.

She was not staying for dinner. She had arrangements of her own. She had come by to bring flowers from her garden in exchange for a large portion of soup, which Edgar's grandniece was carefully ladling from pot to pot. We had arrived early because Edgar had promised to tell stories he had not told before, and his niece was also eager to hear them. I had regained that day some of my long-lost social ease, perhaps because the old man and I had been talking excitedly on our way over to the city. Some time during the early years of the century he had been offered a painted watercolor postcard by a shabby man hawking his own work in front of the Vienna city hall. Many years later he thought he recognized the man as Adolf Hitler, who had been living in the men's barracks in Vienna at the time. "Only think," the old man had said to me with a significant nod as we pulled up near the house of his grandniece, "if we should take seriously the sublimating power of art. Then if the Academy of Fine Arts had not twice rejected him, who knows? Maybe we would today have Adolf the artist, instead of Adolf the killer of Jews. Or suppose on that day I had bought his watercolor. Perhaps we would have exchanged a friendly glance, we might have shaken hands, who is to say? Could the history of the world be changed by a sympathetic encounter of this kind between strangers? *Ach nein,*" he concluded with a vigorous shake of his head as we entered the house, "but this is the kind of thinking that you find sometimes growing in the head of an old man."

We had walked into a large vestibule with an ornate mirror, pegs for coats, benches for changing from outdoor to indoor shoes, which were provided. And there at the end of the corridor was Hadamar, in a white tailored suit, wondering how to get the soup out to the car without spilling it on herself. She looked all lit up that day. Was it because the estranged husband, who wandered about in the world collecting rare manuscripts, had decided to show up? She had changed her hair. It had been long and softly curling the first time we met. Now, with a sharp, angular bob, she looked even more proud than the first time, perhaps momentarily haughty, as once again she seemed not to recognize me and then she did.

I sprang forward to help Hadamar lift the kettle of soup. I must have done it with a playful, courtly air. Everyone was looking at me. Hadamar tipped her head, flashing me that ravishing smile of hers, made a sweeping gesture with both her hands, opening them helplessly, piteously, to acknowledge her role. And then I was gallantly carrying the heavy pot out to the car. I had become someone I hadn't been for years and years. I scarcely remembered that earlier person, who had climbed trees, fought with the boys in our neighborhood, carried my mother's heavy suitcase in and out of the car, opened the umbrella for my third grade teacher, dashed out into the pouring rain to open the car door for her.

Later Hadamar and I could both look back and remember this

day as the beginning of our friendship, but I have always known our friendship began in silence, months before, when I recognized her as the woman I had always been looking for.

It must have been overcast earlier. When we walked out the door I saw for the first time in years the seductive presence of a world battered by sunlight. We got the soup kettle into the car and secured it in place.

Hadamar was evidently a habitual "fetcher" of food she served but did not cook.

We were laughing at this and then about nothing at all, simply because we had started laughing. In laughter Hadamar let herself be known, as if the two of you were happily drowning together when you laughed, your arms flung around each other, blissfully falling away from inhibition.

"Aunt Edith never stops talking about you," Hadamar threw out, too casually, I thought, as she opened the front door of her car. "Whenever you leave she sits by herself crying quietly. She hasn't cried for years. She says she is renewed, cleansed. Everything forgotten comes back to her. Then she goes quickly to the phone to call her friends to tell them about you."

It took me many months to figure out that Hadamar would say certain things, perhaps those that meant the most to her, as if they were said simply in passing, insignificantly.

I didn't want her to get into the car and drive off, waving exuberantly, as she was sure to do, as if we were old friends preparing to meet a few hours later and there was nothing at stake and no question when we would meet each other again.

"I've always hated to stop laughing," I said in order to have something to say. "When I was in school I was always being sent into the coatroom because I laughed too much."

"And I too, I too," she cried out, taking me by the hands. "Aunt Edith has a stack of notes sent to my mother from my teachers, always complaining about my talking and laughter. We'll get her to show them to us. We'll go through them together."

It was the kind of thing Hadamar would say. It made for an instantaneous closeness, a promise of even greater intimacy to come. It didn't mean she and I would ever go through the notes together, if they existed, which at that time I never doubted.

"Call me," she said. "Or better, drop in. Aunt Edith says you live in the neighborhood?"

But this time she couldn't pull it off. It sounded suddenly not at all casual. It was a kind of suspension, a stopping still, an arrest in our awkward, playful banter.

She was looking at me with an expression I wouldn't have believed possible, not for Hadamar. As if she were beseeching me, pleading with me not to let the friendship drop, to take it up, be sure to follow through, to accept the invitation. Again, this obscure message, this silent cry for help. This time I felt a distinct complicity between us, as if we had already begun to lead two lives, a superficial, irrelevant life in the world, played out against a secret communion, intensely meaningful but un-spoken.

I looked away because I thought she would not like this ex-pression to be seen. But when I looked back it was still there, was even more visible, as if she wanted to make sure I had received the message. I was not to be taken in by her appearance. I was to know her in an intimate dimension of our own. I was shown, in those few moments, how deep the possibility ran.

In those days women had already begun to kiss or embrace each other on fairly slight acquaintance, so it didn't seem unusual when Hadamar moved toward me and very lightly placed her cheek against mine to say good-bye.

7

Friendship moves slowly, cautiously, almost suspiciously when the women involved cannot understand why they would want to be friends. They have nothing in common; therefore, their sense that they are being drawn together makes them uneasy, as if they were in the presence of a mysterious force that is working on them, perhaps even against their will. But for what purpose?

Hadamar Bonheim, a member of boards, committees, foundations, a woman who rose early, was on the move until late at night, a woman who would invariably be hailed and greeted whenever she walked down the street—what could Hadamar Bonheim possibly want from Kim Chernin, who so rarely left her house?

Not that I called her or dropped by. I may have been living in a cave, but I had not lost my sense of social cunning. A woman of her type, worldly, ambitious, used to being courted, would secretly despise anyone who came after her. I seemed to know this instinctively. Therefore, I hung back, I held myself aloof. If she was the one for whom I would change my life, if the time was right, a few weeks, even a few months more or less, would not matter.

I ran into her once at Aunt Edith's house as I was leaving, but she only waved to me from her car. And again another time when I was in the park with Jurgen Linden, a surgeon who had started his practice in Berlin during the early 1900s. He showed me how he had learned to walk with a slight stoop, wearing a padded vest to make his stomach prominent. A young man at the time, he'd been forced to find a way to make himself look old; otherwise he would never have been able to get patients or referrals. He had worn spectacles, although he had perfect sight, and a false beard until his own grew in sufficiently to suggest advanced maturity.

We were feeding squirrels in the arboretum. He put his hand very tenderly on my head, as if I reminded him of someone else. "What is youth?" he asked, in answer to a question I had not posed. "Youth is an invention of the postwar era. When I was young, there was no youth, only immaturity."

He was looking over my head, in the direction of the little bridge. He had begun to smile, to lift his hand in greeting, and I knew at once that he was greeting Hadamar. I didn't have to turn to look, I knew who it was. Later on it sometimes happened that before I could possibly have seen her, or heard her voice, I would know she was present or coming along or would show up in the next moment.

She was walking with several women her own age, all of them well dressed, their voices lowered. I saw her from the corner of my eye as they passed the lawn in front of the duck pond. There were black swans on the water. I thought Hadamar had seen me, too, looked away quickly, then pretended to be surprised that I was there. They all stopped to say hello to the old man, who rose promptly, bowed to them, then raised Hadamar's hand to his lips.

"I see you have met my friend Kim Chernin," she said, in that deep, caressing voice of hers. "But without my intervention? I thought the two of you would have much in common."

He and I looked sheepishly at each other, as if we had failed to realize we had come together because of Hadamar. She took control of a situation so promptly, created an impression of intimacy so quickly, one immediately surrendered one's own sense of reality to enter hers. And why not? If I was right about her, wouldn't she soon surrender a very great deal to enter mine?

I too stood up, because I was being introduced to the other women, who seemed to have heard of me, to be pleased to meet me, to have something to tell me, perhaps about a distant cousin with a past I would like to record.

Everyone looked at me expectantly, as if waiting for me to come up with something special. I took Hadamar's hand in mine, bent low the way the old man had done, raised her fingers close to my lips, then drew myself erect.

As a boy, it seemed, I was a rascal: a bit wild, arrogantly sure of myself. I could take for granted how much I would be admired. I was not surprised when everyone laughed and applauded. I had evidently acquired a reputation as a charming eccentric who might do or say anything. It might have been Hadamar herself, who was gazing at me as if I were a prize cat, or Aunt Edith, or Edgar Rosenwasser, or even the old woman from Prague who had been a close friend of Kafka's sister—any one of them might have said nice things about me because I was genuinely happy in their company. I probably seemed to have a quirky, sunny, spontaneous disposition. But nothing could have been further from the truth. It was only now, now with the appearance of the boy. His coming had saved me from myself, brought me back to life, carried me out into the world—if only the world of ghosts, displaced persons, and shadows.

I had held on to Hadamar's hand, or perhaps she had held on to mine. I noticed the very light pressure of her knuckles against my lips, a touch so intimate it made insignificant the most passionate kisses I had known so far. I did not want to give up this new sensation, or the sharp pressure of her ring on my lips, or the fragile musk of tea rose perfume. I didn't think she noticed until she gave me a sharp warning look. Or perhaps it was a look of dazed recognition or even fear. But in the next moment she had gracefully freed her hand from mine, lifted both hands up above her shoulders, as if to give the old man and me her blessing, kissed him lightly on the cheek, waved good-bye to me, and the four of them were off, heads bent together, urgently discussing.

But at the gate to the arboretum she suddenly turned back, took a few steps toward us, and called out gaily, "Be sure to call. Remember? You promised."

She could have been speaking to either one of us, but it was clear she was speaking to me. She couldn't afford to leave it to chance. It meant too much to her. Was this the sign I had been waiting for?

I didn't call for a long time. Weeks must have passed before I called, and then it was on the day I knew my marriage to Max was over. I had begun to understand that once the call was made, Hadamar and I would have reached a crossroads. There, I would lose or win her; it would happen violently, a choice would have to be made. It was, I felt, like everything else between Hadamar and me: we were drawn along by it, as if we had stepped into an undertow and could only clasp hands and be drawn out together. Friendship between women can be that journey, and Hadamar knew this as well as I.

She was waiting for us on the porch the first time Max and I went to her house for a Sabbath meal. It was Aunt Edith, not Hadamar, who had invited us. But it was Hadamar who ran down the steps to walk back with us, drawing her arms through both our own although she had not met Max before and I had still not called her.

Aunt Edith was waiting at the door. The little girls were there, too, several tall boys in yarmulkes, the golden retriever, who came over to sniff, an old wolfhound who kept his distance but eyed us narrowly. Hadamar seemed to be introducing us as long-lost family to the portly man with a red beard and a capo in his shirt pocket, to the artist-cousin who did monumental sculptures in Tokyo, to the women I had already met in the park, who were cousins or aunts or in-laws and served on committees with Hadamar. She introduced us to a very slender woman with a pale, pinched, suffering face, a thoracic surgeon, who turned out to be the mother of the two girls who were hanging on Hadamar, fighting over possession of her right hand, the space in front of her, the chair next to her at the table. The three boys were better behaved, perhaps conscious of their more serious dignity as members of the community now old enough to speak responsible blessings over the wine. Edgar Rosenwasser was there with his beard trimmed and his bald head gleaming. I was introduced to two elderly women, who might have been sisters and were currently staying with Hadamar. They seemed to have a close relationship to the elder of the three boys, but it was never easy to determine the exact degree of relation between any two people at an intimate Bonheim gathering.

That night, we had been invited, for the first time, into the inner circle of Bonheim society, a group made up of doctors and lawyers and professors and dentists, collectors and amateur artists. The men were gourmet cooks, the women had professions or ran a business. They attended the opera on Saturday nights, having thoroughly studied the scores and librettos; they had the best seats in the house from patiently moving forward year after year of subscription tickets. They did not drink champagne during intermission; they had tables reserved with coffee and cake, made a large, buzzing, excited gathering that spread out over most of the downstairs lobby, where the virtues and faults of the performers were meticulously, unerringly discussed between tables. Later on I went often with Hadamar, who had kept her subscription after she and her husband had separated. Before we became friends she used to give the tickets away. But when she found out I loved opera, we went practically every Saturday during that season, from early fall until December, usually dining out after the opera with others I had by that time come to know well. Twice in December we had dinner alone together, and once we stayed until we were politely asked to leave the Hayes Street Grill, after drinking a good six glasses of amaretto and eating a large number of shared crèmes caramels. There were nights like that, when we were at ease together, as if we had been meeting and toasting each other and whispering together for so long we could take our giddy happiness simply for granted.

But during that first Sabbath dinner, seated a good distance away from Hadamar down the long table, next to Edgar and the boy who blessed the wine and across from Max, I felt the conspicuous, almost urgent tension that ran from Hadamar to me and always seemed to establish a bond where none seemed apparent, to make me act when I would otherwise have remained quiet.

After dinner, the chairs were drawn back, the portly, bearded man played the guitar, Aunt Edith clapped and tapped her foot, Edgar Rosenwasser offered his arm, Edith grabbed one of the girls, who grabbed the tall boy with down on his lip, who grabbed the mother-surgeon, who came along into the slow step-cross-step in a large, moving circle around the table. Everyone who passed the head of the table grabbed Hadamar by the arm; she refused, always laughing. "Hadamar never dances," one of the small girls confided in me, as we became partners briefly before we were spun apart.

Hadamar never dances? Even her most casual gesture was highly stylized, distinctly graceful. She had small hands with exquisite, slender fingers, long legs, a modeled head held proudly on a long, sinuous neck. She wore silver bracelets, her eyes glowed and sparkled even when she was leaning on an elbow at the head of a table, refusing to dance. And somehow, perhaps precisely because of this refusal, the entire gathering seemed to circle around her, as if she had set us in motion with a flicker of will.

Hadamar never dances? But Hadamar will dance because I ask her. Was that what I had decided? Aunt Edith and Edgar Rosenwasser had dropped out of the circle. I was moving fast because the music and clapping were growing faster, I was spinning my way up to the head of the table, stopping suddenly with a low, sweeping bow as Hadamar slowly, hesitantly, then exuberantly crossed her arm through mine, as if I had released her from a spell.

It was the boy again. For him, a question simply of jumping and spinning, putting my hands around her waist, stamping my feet when we came to one end of the table, whooping loudly at the other end, freed entirely from inhibition and social embarrassment. I had a right to court the woman I loved. Because I assumed this, she responded; because I did not hesitate, she danced with me. That comic bow of mine had swept Stevens and his habitual disapproval out of the picture, at least for now. I had drawn her up into a raucous, easy-going abandon. The speed, the whirl, the impetuous rush of movement must have made her forget she had never danced with a woman before. I could tell, from her reluctance to let go, how much she loved the hard pressure of my hand on her waist. I knew how completely she gave herself over to the force by which I spun her away from me, as she looked over her shoulder with an expression of bewildered joy, before I drew her back in, skipping, eager to return to me.

That was another occasion when we laughed so hard we

could not stop. But it was not the first time our experience seemed to divide into that thrilling, raucous deception of the social world, while in some other degree of relation we were already sitting up late at the window of her upstairs room, as we would soon do, scarcely talking as it became morning and we were flung far from ourselves into strange and unpredictable transfigurations.

8

There was a silver dog tied to the parking meter. He had an erect, noble head, a short-haired coat that looked as if it had been recently polished. He gave the impression that his restraint was an unnecessary indignity. His owner would merely have had to say the word; he would have waited patiently without stirring from the spot, forever.

There was a tall man with light brown hair. He was coming down the stairs from a camera store, a woman was walking beside him, they both seemed to know my companion, they were moving quickly toward us, smiling, eager to greet us.

He and I were introduced to each other: Max Singer, Kim Chernin.

This is a story I told to Hadamar when we became friends.

In the excitement I must have stepped back into the street. A car was pulling up too fast next to the curb. Max Singer sprang forward to catch me by the arm. He put his arm around my shoulder when I started shaking. So that's how we met, that's how it happened.

Mowens, the silver dog, had pricked up his ears and was star-ing fixedly in the direction of the offending car. There were hefty apologies as the driver came toward us with a shuffling, embar-rassed step. But Mowens was disinclined to accept these excuses. He bared his fangs and gave a modulated growl.

Thom, my companion, took my arm; he was ready to move on. He and Max were both members of an organization called Physicians for Social Responsibility. They had met recently at a demonstration in support of the grape pickers who were on strike in the Salinas Valley. Thom was frowning. Was it because of the way Max Singer sprang out to save me, so protectively, so gallantly?

As we walked off, Thom and I toward the harbor, Max and his girlfriend on into town, I looked back over my shoulder. Max had looked back too, so it didn't surprise me when Thom and I received a call the next morning. We were invited to a New Year's Eve party on Max's houseboat.

Thom was reluctant to go, but we went. He put his hand heavily on my shoulder as we walked up the rickety plank and climbed up over the high steps into the boat. There was a crowd our own age, mostly under thirty, young professionals, artists, writers, photographers, a group in which I felt immediately at home, while Thom seemed unnecessarily reserved and quiet, although he was a well-known local figure whom people imme-diately recognized.

Max was sitting up on the back of a threadbare armchair, which looked as if it had done years of service for the silver dog. The room was fairly dark; there was a light in the kitchen, a few candles by the windows. The woman from the day before came over to sit next to him. Thom brought me a glass of red wine.

Max had been playing union songs I knew from my childhood. People would sing a verse or two, drop out, hum along, start clapping. I knew the words of every song. From that moment he was playing only for me, and I thought Max Singer was the sort of man any woman would want to spend the rest of her life with, no questions asked. He tried Yiddish lullabies, I knew them. He played a Russian folk song I had learned at the Youth Festival in Moscow. We both knew songs in Spanish from the Lincoln Brigade. Sometimes I sang off-key and he brought me back again. When he couldn't find a single song I didn't know, he put the guitar aside, jumped down from the back of the chair, came over to kneel in front of me, so tall that I still had to look up to him.

Our parents were radical Jews from Eastern Europe. Sholem Aleichem was Max's distant cousin. We knew the same stories, and I still always forgot the end of them so that my father could tell them suspensefully one more time. Later on, this capacity—to listen eagerly to the same story no matter how many times it was told—came in handy with Max, too.

What a radiant youthfulness he had back then. Blue eyes,

light brown hair, a fine, high-bridged nose in a face showing vulnerability, sensitivity, intelligence. There was a perceptible gaiety in his eyes, as if he were the guardian of a mysterious well-being. He was without doubt the most beautiful man I had ever seen. I thought so then and in this regard my opinion of him has never changed. He was not yet thirty and I was certainly not the only woman who looked back at him when he passed on the street. We danced some and had to stop dancing because of how much we were talking. Thom wanted to go home, Max persuaded us to stay for a glass of champagne. I managed to get into trouble that night, too, when we went outside to watch the fireworks. I jumped up on the railing to see better and would have been just fine because I knew how to move fast and had good balance. But Thom was startled. He fumbled for my hand, I began to wobble, and Max caught me.

There was not much danger. The tide was moving out and by that time the crucial chord had already been struck. I took certain kinds of risks, which sometimes worked out and sometimes didn't. Max was the man who would be there to keep me safe. Later on, he'd be the one to whom I would always return when things didn't work out elsewhere. That chord would ring down through the next twelve years of our relationship, and when it no longer sounded, the relationship shattered.

That is how I explained it to Hadamar on the day I finally called her, when I knew my relationship with Max had come to an end. How many times he had been there with flowers at the airport, although the plane was always hours late and the flowers had begun to wither by the time I returned from my aborted trip. I called him when I was stuck in a hippie commune up the coast and didn't want to stay and was suddenly afraid to drive home alone. Whenever I called he would hesitate only a moment. It was an authentic hesitation. He had to make a rapid-fire calculation whether to be hurt again. Then he would decide to break off a casual relationship he had formed, or take time off from work, or come to rescue me, sometimes halfway across the world.

A lot of women back then used to think life wasn't worth living without a man. Hadamar was one of those women. She could never figure what I meant when I said my relationship with Max had lived itself out. During all my cave-dwelling years, he and I had been waiting for me to emerge, to take up a real life beside him, but that's not what happened. We had enough in common to have worked out many kinds of bonds. But neither one of us wanted it any other way. Some relationships are like that, the theme is locked in place. If you don't want to play it, find someone else. Between Kim Chernin and Max Singer things could not have been different.

That's the way I saw it then. I saw everything as prefigured and fated, as if our lives were an old story we were simply repeating, perhaps most of all when we seemed to be making them up. For months I had been waiting for my relationship with Max to be over so that my whole life could change and my friendship with Hadamar could begin. It would happen when it must and that's how it happened.

I had been waiting for Max to come home. It was one of those days. They are hard to describe because most people don't know what it's like when time stops passing. I used to call him at work to discuss the eternal duration of an intolerable moment and he would come home as soon as he could. But one day he forgot. I called him again at his office; he wasn't there. I went out to wait for him in front of the house. I went back inside to call his friend Jim, who hadn't heard from him since that morning. I got in the car, drove around some, passed by our café on Telegraph Avenue, drove over to our swim club.

As I drove, I could see perfectly that time was passing for other people. They seemed to be living out their lives on the other side of a spun-glass barrier. Sunlight fell on them, time moved among them, their world was alive. But I stood in a solitary, anguished shadow and only Max knew how to release me. All he had to do was come home, put his arms around me, let me cry, and I would feel better. No one else had this key; he alone possessed it. He had never before failed to come.

I didn't expect him to be at the swim club, but I had to do something, so I went to look. I spotted him at once, lying peacefully in the sun reading a newspaper. He never saw me, I never told him about it. I stood near the gate, leaning quietly against the Coke machine, and took in the impression of his suddenly revealed, profound indifference, in spite of what he believed about how much he loved me.

It wasn't my decision. It had to happen, although we would not admit it back then and he cried about it more than I did. I must have stood there for a good half-hour, shading my eyes from the sun in that sudden audible silencing of our bond. Time had returned to me. With time, the sense of the unbearable died away. He no longer wanted to rescue me. And I? Was it possible? I now no longer needed to be rescued?

I went home, I walked fast into the house, picked up the phone, dialed information, called Hadamar, who told me the shortcut to her house, and so I ran all the way there without stopping.

Nothing is ever clear when clarity is needed. What might have been said doesn't get said because it will only be known when it's too late. I was still at the very beginning of my friendship with Hadamar, the most brilliant, seductive, lost, ambitious woman I had ever met, contradictory, elusive, capable of sudden, quickly vanishing passages of intimacy that bound you to her and made you forever hope they would happen again.

The door was ajar when I arrived. I knocked lightly, she called for me to come in. She was sitting on the floor in a small room with French doors opening onto the garden. She was pouring tea into small cups; the tea was steaming as I sat down across from her on a flat, embroidered pillow like the one on which she was sitting, her legs crossed, her right hand resting lightly on her thigh. I would have expected to feel shy, this first time we were alone together. But everything kept feeling as if it was working out the way it was supposed to, the way it had happened before, and we, who were living it, might also have been said merely to be remembering.

I took my cup of tea. I told her about Max and the nature of destiny, about the love that wakes people to that singular, spellbound soul seeking its beloved through centuries, through eternities. She looked girlish, bewildered, she clapped her hands with pleasure, she drank my cup of tea, poured another, gave it back to me, put her hand on my arm, once, lightly, laughing, then she was listening to me I thought more seriously than anyone had before and then she was crying, very quietly.

I felt a wild vertigo, a snapping of roots, a free plunge into pure desire, heedless, owning no responsibility. I had chosen myself as potent and invulnerable. I sprang up and took one step toward her. I knew the moment had come. I crouched down next to her and then, when she didn't stop crying, I took her face between my hands and looked at her as if I were going to kiss her. Things like that were possible with Hadamar, who put her head on my shoulder as if nothing could be more natural than this uproar between two people who had never had tea alone together before.

Part 2

9

I wonder if anyone will ever tell all there is to be told about women. Women who are married, or mothers, or who meet for the first time as grandmothers often mean more to each other than anyone has ever meant to either one of them—yes, even more than husbands and children. But this truth tends to be kept a collective secret.

Women can be close without being sexual, sexual without being passionate, passionate without being erotic, erotic without making a physical claim to the beloved, and they can be all these together with such subtle sensual passage from laughter to confession to whispered intimacy that no one in the world could say where friendship leaves off and love begins.

This mysteriousness makes every relationship between two women into an exploration of terra incognita. What goes on in every moment women are alone together is taking place beyond what is culturally named and acknowledged. Because it is subtle, silent, undefined and enjoys its secrecy, the true nature of women's relationships is often kept hidden, even from women themselves.

Women have a way of laughing when they are together that no man has ever heard. The moment his presence is known or even sensed, this laughter undergoes a marked transformation. It becomes girlish or secretive or lighthearted or coy, but never does it allow itself to ring out with the sheer pleasure in each other's company that had originally inspired it. There is no problem about all this when two women, who have grown fond of each other, are equally ignorant of what might be possible between them. Best of all, perhaps, is the slow mutual dawning of this possibility between two women who are waking up together, then initiating each other. It is not a tragedy that men generally, or the culture as a whole, remain ignorant of these awakenings and make up for their ignorance by imagining that nothing exists between women that men don't already know. This only keeps the secret safe from inevitable intrusions, envy, and disruptions.

The difficulty arises when one of the women wakes up first, comes to know something the other woman does not know, cannot afford to know, or is reluctant to recognize, while yet holding (oh yes) as tightly as possible to the other, to whom she cannot give herself but whom she can also not let go.

The wakeful one knows something worth knowing. The one who is not yet awake cannot fail to notice this. She wants the knowing the other has achieved, but maybe she doesn't like the risk involved. Perhaps she believes she will find out through the other, by watching her, by keeping her close. Probably the reluctant one is fascinated by these changes in her friend she sees taking place before her eyes because her friend has fallen in love, although the hesitant one is reluctant to admit this falling in love has to do with her. Yet she senses the ardent awakening of the other's desire as it begins to hover over her, protective, passionate, subtle, ever watchful.

Is the sleeper awaking, too? Should the lover give her a gentle shake? Why not take her hand and draw her along with you for a step or two to see how she responds? But what if the knowledge you have, the hazardous knowing that this friendship has fallen in love, wakes the chaste sleepwalker too harshly? Therefore, caution: spend every moment you can with her, sit by her bed telling her stories when she falls asleep at night, but do nothing to wake her. Don't let her know you have found the way to cross over within yourself into a life as a boy. Wait quietly, treasure the unexpected askesis of loving a woman who is waking more slowly than you, but is by every sign and indication moving toward you.

10

Do you ever feel that you want to take some enormous step, do something wild and irresponsible and change your whole life?" Hadamar asks me as I turn a corner too fast, throwing her over against me, then sharply back to her own side of the car. These confidential moods come up suddenly, out of nowhere, unexpectedly. Usually they disappear as abruptly as they have set in. Therefore, I am constantly on guard not to miss their arrivals or departures.

I park on a dark neighborhood street, where Hadamar uses the driveway of an abandoned church a few doors down from her favorite restaurant. She knows the cook and can trust him to turn out something special for her and her guests. The place is small, the food is very good, there is a wood-burning stove in the corner of the room near our table, and I like to think of this place as uniquely ours. But in fact Hadamar comes here frequently, and not always with me.

She reaches back to squeeze my hand as we are going down the stairs. "Well, do you?"

I have been sifting through her words to see if they have been spoken in general, in one of her flights of exuberance about nothing in particular, or have specific relevance for me.

"Of course I want to change my whole life," I say as I open the heavy door and let her pass in front of me into the restaurant. "Every morning and all through the day and every night I'm thinking about changing my life."

"Yes," she says, as if she knows exactly what I'm talking about.

"And especially so since I met you."

"Sweet," she says to me indifferently, lifting her hand to acknowledge the waiter in a formal jacket, pleated shirt, and faded blue jeans, who is winking at her. "Especially so since you met me?"

She says this curiously, as if she has no idea an intimate relationship has been growing up between us. On other occasions she seems to know very well that we are important to each other, and she will even say something about it herself. But the next time I meet up with her, expecting some continuity, some evolution in this closeness, she seems to have forgotten all about it, as if it had never taken place.

Nevertheless I am not going to back off. "Yes, since I met you, especially. Does that surprise you?"

I can usually count on her to answer a direct challenge, and she does this time, too.

"I'm aware that our friendship means a lot to you. But you

have to understand something, Kim. It means just as much to me."

This takes my breath away. It is said in a hushed voice as we slip into our seats, side by side, at a table built into the corner near the copper wood-burning stove, where now, on a cold summer evening, a fire of kindling and small pinecones is burning.

We are in a wine cellar reached by steep stairs and a quick passage through the mahogany-paneled bar where crates of wine are stored. The waiter brings her favorite wine, a crisp Chardonnay from the Anderson Valley. He pours a small amount into a glass for her, she smiles and nods, he sips it himself with a light salute. They are, as always, pleased by their little ritual, in which Hadamar demonstrates her ability to invite social transgression.

And now there is an odd bustling at our table, in which the wonderful words she has just spoken, which seem to carry so much meaning, have trouble finding a place. I have observed this before; I have almost grown used to it. She has told me how much I mean to her and then moved on so fast to something else I'm left wondering whether she ever spoke the words.

I pour her wine. She takes a sip, then raises her glass to my lips. The message is clear, or is it? We'll drink from the same glass of wine, heads bent toward each other, in the intimate haze Hadamar seems to create unthinkingly, as if it were spun out by the force of some erotic element in her personality for which she has never been asked to take responsibility.

I know all this about her by now. Nevertheless, I believe she is trying to reach something in herself, some capacity for transformation or surrender, that makes her want to change her entire life, as she has said, however lightly the words themselves might have been spoken tonight.

"Hadamar, tell me something," I say, pouring my own glass of wine. It is a deliberate effort to resist the shadow-play of intimacy, to bring us into the real thing. "Do you really want to change your life? Does our friendship really mean as much to you as it does to me?"

But now I see that I have fully engaged her. Her dark eyes concentrate, meet mine, allow themselves to look startled.

"Do I?" she asks, as if wondering for the first time if she does. "Do I want to change my life? Somehow, I feel that I do. Yes, I do. I'm tired of waiting for Stevens to change his mind or make up his mind or not make up his mind. Sometimes, when I'm falling asleep I hear my own name. 'Hadamar,' something says, so clearly, with a mysterious, silver intensity. I sit right up in bed feeling that I'm being called, that I should be responding. But what is this call? What could the response be? Somehow," she says in a lowered voice, shifting her eyes away from mine, "I feel that you know something about these things. Do you?"

It's not the first time she has seemed almost desperate in the urgency of what she is trying to work out. She looks now like someone who has been tossed down and has been falling from far away, and only I am there to break her fall.

"Look here, Hadamar. For me the sense of a new beginning always seems to have something, even a great deal, to do with you."

"As if we were both supposed to start out on a journey together? You feel that, too? I can't tell you how often I have the impression I've been waiting to meet up with you for my whole life. As if everything else were only a rehearsal, a preparation."

She says this with a dreamy, preoccupied air, somewhat curiously, as if her own words have taken her by surprise, so that she might in the next moment wake up and wonder, Did I say that?

The waiter is looking at her impatiently, waiting for an acknowledgment as he places the careful salad of greens and goat cheese in front of us.

I can't wait for him to go away. I'm afraid he will interrupt this confession that seems so precarious, that has been so long, I feel, in coming.

She nods to him vaguely, then gazes absently at her plate. He shrugs, turns away; she looks over at me, seems startled to see me, catches hold of my hand.

"Do you really know what all this is about? Really?"

The weeks we have spent together, talking daily on the phone, going for walks, running errands, stopping by each other's houses, sitting up late at night talking, going to restaurants, meeting her friends, could now, at this very moment, stumble over into what they have meant. Someone could say, This is about the way we feel for each other. This is about, oh I don't know, this is about leaving everything else behind. This is about finding out what we mean to each other. This is about falling in love.

Am I going to say these things? As a boy, I would definitely say them. I keep waiting for myself to speak. Now. Now or never. No, not now, later. Now it will only scare her away. The boy version of myself comes and goes as it pleases. Sometimes I think this has to do with Hadamar, sometimes with the fact that I haven't yet left Max. The boy would put an arm around her, draw her close, say something possessive. But as a boy I would never be able to make my way through the subtle passages of intimacy and withdrawal through which she takes me.

"Sometimes I think I do know what all this is about," I say with an uneasy sense of evasion. I need a woman's wits about me now, an ability to read silences, interpret casual gestures, pick up cues that haven't been given.

She moves over very close to me, as if expecting me to speak softly or even to whisper. When I remain silent, she laughs confidingly. "You want me to guess?"

For a second I think the moment has come. But then something in her laughter makes me suddenly aware she has no idea where this conversation has been leading. Or maybe even that she knew a second ago, but as the confessional moment has drawn near, she has danced aside with the very gesture that seems to make us so intimate. This is not the laughter of a woman who expects a declaration of love. There is something too light about it, offhand, seamlessly merry. It lacks the edge of anxiety anyone would feel at a moment like this, unless of course it was an old game in which she was already highly practiced.

Is it possible?

The waiter comes over to see how we're doing. We haven't touched our food. She looks up at him without the least sign of embarrassment. "We can't eat," she says in her charming way. "We're in the midst of a great suspense. We're playing a guessing game."

"Oh," he says, more cheerful now. "When you want to know, just ask me. I'll let you in on our most secret ingredients."

By the time we are alone again, and Hadamar picks up her fork, to separate out a piece of Belgian endive with its sprinkle of black pepper, our earlier conversation has vanished. Now it is I who feel that someone has tossed me down from a great height, but it won't be Hadamar who breaks my fall.

She eats slowly, speculatively. She nudges me on the elbow, to make me eat, too. "It's raspberry vinegar," she says tentatively, "mixed with brown rice vinegar, a touch of miso, and perhaps, perhaps even a—"

"Hadamar," I say impatiently.

She smiles her dazzling smile.

"Eat, eat," she says soothingly. "We have the whole night to talk. When we have had dinner I'll take you to a place you've never been before. No, I assure you, you don't know it, Stevens discovered it a few years ago, people like us don't go there, but you and I will go and we'll have our talk."

She seems to be telling me that the restaurant is too public for the conversation we've been about to have. That means she must know what the conversation was about and is only postponing it until she finds a better time and place.

"Open your mouth," she says. "I'll have to feed you if you're not going to eat."

This imperative tenderness immediately reassures me. In its own way it is a declaration of love, playful only because of our circumstance. I let her feed me a delicate leaf of romaine lettuce with a morsel of white cheese. The way she looks at me now, in her wry and complicit silence, seems a very private way of making love, as blatantly as possible, in a public setting.

"That's good," she murmurs as I open my mouth. "But I never imagined you would be so obedient."

I know what people mean when they say their head swims or they feel faint or giddy or can't catch their breath. But this sensation is immediately swept away by a wondrous joy.

We have already said what we have been trying to say. Every expression, the radiant look in her deep-set eyes, the outrageous way she goes on feeding me, leaning lightly against my shoulder, says a thousand times what words would not have been able to say. It's my hesitation and confusion that are holding us back, my cautious decoding of every word and gesture. Hadamar has already come more than halfway to meet me and invite me. All I have to do now is believe in this and respond. But the boy has no way to get in through this sticky web of subtlety, inclination, and evasion.

11

A long walkway winds out between the bay and a small yacht harbor near the freeway. She's right; I have never been here before. In a late dusk, there is an odd light slanting in through the gathering fog, so that the port of Oakland, across the water, is here and there pieced out in a luminous, almost garish whiteness.

I have driven past this place hundreds, thousands of times on my way to the city and would never have thought to stop. I have always thought of the place as a usurper, hijacking the view of the city and the mountains for the use of tourists. There are hotels, and expensive restaurants with bad food, built up on the landfill where nothing commercial should exist.

"Just wait," Hadamar says. "You're right as far as that goes. But Stevens was always finding places like this, off the beaten track because they seem to be so much a part of the beaten track, until some indigenous wildness gets hold of them. You'll see, you won't believe where you are. Restaurants, hotels, gas stations, freeway are going to be left far, far behind. If you still believe, five minutes from now, that we are in a place you know well and recognize . . ."

"What? What then? And if I do believe?"

"We'll have to see. Not that I'm worried. I know what lies ahead."

She has been thoroughly at ease since we left the restaurant, deliberately tossing directions at me when it's almost too late, laughing heartily when I manage a turn in the last moment, with a sharp spin that throws us together. The control of our relationship seems to have passed over to her, as if she has understood my awkwardness and will now take things in hand herself. This has made me feel very young and shy. (Great, a shy boy! Who needs him?) It is a new and unexpected configuration, as if I were out cruising for the first time with the older sister of a high school chum.

As we walk, she takes my arm. I'm carrying the windbreakers and two scarves she keeps in the trunk of her car. At first our silence seems promising, as if we're figuring out how to say what we have promised to say.

There is a yacht harbor on our right, moody in the twilight, the sailboats moored, rocking, restless.

It seems to be getting dark fast.

"It is late summer," she agrees, in her grand manner. "We have grown used to long days that have surreptitiously been drawing in." But I'm afraid it will get too dark and too cold before we have managed to talk.

Our silence leaves me time to probe and wonder about her every gesture, the passing expressions of her face. The dark green lapping waves are beginning to hit hard against the rocks bordering our path. The wind is up. We are close to the water, only a few feet away; there is a sweet smell of heather and salt and then we are past the last building, a seaside restaurant, which begins to take on the forlorn, far-flung look that Hadamar has promised, as if we were walking at the far point of a forgotten island. The path narrows and threads between ice plant and cypress trees; we turn the corner and the place is seized by an unexpected wildness. Berkeley has disappeared behind a stand of cypress; Mount Tamalpais, across the bay, in its haughty wrapping of mist, gives the impression of a far-off sacred mountain. There are a few sailboats turning back to shore; the bridges are slowly removing themselves behind night and fog. We could be anywhere.

We have reached a bench some feet from a solitary street light, our destination. From here, if this mist were not so heavy, all three bridges would be visible, charging across the bay on their perpetual missions of connection. It is the sort of place a connoisseur would choose, the right place for conversation, if only our conversation would begin. Hadamar takes my hand, leans lightly against my shoulder, and steps up onto the bench. I read this gesture with my entire body. The boy's shyness has just been replaced by a virile caution. Instantly, I feel taller than I felt a moment ago, leaner and stronger, as if I have become a protective presence, as if my strength, fearlessness, vigilance will make possible this perilous rendezvous in a forsaken place as it grows dark.

She walks along the bench, holding my hand. We say nothing. I look at her from the corners of my eyes, wondering what she's up to. She seems relaxed, somewhat dreamy, as if she had forgotten the reason we have come here. I can see her clearly in the subdued light from the street lamp, but I cannot organize the impressions for which I am continually at watch. Is she at peace with me because we have already had our explanation? Have we passed beyond the need for talk and declaration? Is she one of those women who will glide imperceptibly into love, gesture building upon gesture until an ultimate intimacy is reached?

My body is charged with partial impulses, quickly defeated gestures. I can imagine springing up onto the bench next to her, wrapping my arms around her. It seems an easy matter, so far as my body is concerned, to draw her down into my arms. It is impossible to imagine refusal, hesitation. The silent inclination that moves from her to me speaks welcome and surrender.

And now suddenly she looks very sad. "On our honeymoon," she says, hunching her shoulders as she steps down from the bench, "we stayed only in farmhouses and small inns, where Stevens knew we could get the freshest eggs, butter, homemade breads. I can't tell you what it's like to travel with him. He's a connoisseur of hidden places, neglected landscapes, old churches with frescoes that haven't been retouched, mountain villages in which the boys' choir sings with incredible purity. He was a poet of the small and irrelevant, the overlooked, the unimportant. For me, a whole world of cultivated sensations was opening, in which I seemed to live with complete ease, as if I were returning to my own natural habitat. But my family never liked him. They found him effete, superior, affected. Even Aunt Edith didn't like him, and she, you know, can take in almost everything."

Could the world I offered compare with his? Could I be for her a connoisseur of an inner landscape that would seem as new to her and as fascinating as the hidden world he had offered? She had spoken about Stevens before. I had understood this confessional gesture, our sharing of secrets, this saying of things that she wouldn't have said to anyone else, even to him, as an acknowledged intimacy. This time, although I didn't want to believe it, the whole speech seemed a subterfuge, as if she had run off from what was happening between us into this old, familiar grief, which must seem so much less dangerous to her than I was, sitting next to her on the wooden bench.

I put the windbreaker on her shoulders and tied the scarf around her neck. She didn't seem to notice. Her eyes held mine, as if demanding that I stay close to her in her urgency. As if, I thought, we had to go through this one more time to get where we were going.

"Where did it go wrong? Did it go wrong? Who was to blame? Is anyone to blame when these things happen? We seemed so happy. I'm not a person who usually misses these things, especially when they matter. I don't even know when it began. I try, but I can't fix the day, the time, I can't capture the transition. Kim, are you listening?" She grabbed my arm. "You have to listen. Don't imagine I've told you any of this before. We were happy, we traveled about for years, he taught me what he knew, a kind of seeing of the small and undistinguished I had never come across before. We visited collectors, we stayed in out-of-the-way places, I was ecstatic the whole time in that eccentric world of his, that infinitely exquisite world of little-known music and ruined estates, visiting people like him in cities it would never occur to anyone else to visit. And then suddenly we weren't happy anymore. He was aloof, distant, unreachable in a way I'd never imagined he could be, strangely fastidious, as if my very presence were a trial to him, so that then I was desperate to win him back, to make him notice me. I don't imagine you have ever lost yourself like that. No, I'm sure you haven't. Not like that, not out of desperation for another person's love or affection or even, finally, simply for them to notice you, to see that you are still there . . ."

I had seen her cry before, her face still and forsaken, but this time I understood that she was not crying because of grief. They were tears of self-reproach and mortification and I was afraid that in the next moment she would be furious at me for having understood them.

"I am a proud woman," she said in a muffled voice. "You have no idea how proud I am. I sometimes think I cannot stop waiting for him to come back, because I am plotting my revenge. All love, all longing, all desire was burnt up ages ago by this obsession. That is what I have wanted to tell you."

Her face was fierce, her dark eyes blazing. She had taken both my hands in hers, clenching them against her knees. I felt that I should be moved, startled, deeply stirred by her confession. I felt nothing. A wooden disbelief seemed to settle on me, as if I had just witnessed a magnificent performance that would turn out, after all, to be a consummate evasion.

"You say nothing," she said after a time. "It's not like you. You always have something to say, you are always delicate and re-sponsive."

"This obsession you describe? Forgive me," I said in a husky voice, "but somehow I can't believe in it."

She looked at me with surprise, curious about what I had to say. I imagined a hidden respect for me in her eyes, as if she were secretly proud of me for not being taken in. "No, I don't believe in it," I said, with no effort to hide my anger. "If you had told me this story two years ago I would have known you were telling me the truth. But by now it has become an old story—yes, even if you have never told it to anyone else before, it's old and irrelevant. This obsession is nothing but a way you've found of refusing to go on, to risk a new life, some new transformation or momentum. You fall back into it as steadily as rainwater running downhill. I'm not impressed by it."

If I had planned a strategy I couldn't have made a better move. Incredibly, she threw back her head and laughed. I had taken her by surprise, responded to her in a way she would not have predicted. She stood up, as if some way had to be found to contain her excitement. She walked quickly over to the street light, turned back with an eager expression. "Do you know all that? Am I as clear as that to you? You seem to know me better than I know myself. Far better. I no longer need this obsession if I'm willing to move on? But what does that mean, to move on? Move on where, to what? Does it have something to do with you?"

I shrugged, suddenly exhausted by the hours of suspense, fagged out from the concentration I had brought to the slightest movement of her hands, the tilt of a raised eyebrow, the imperceptible degrees of closeness between our knees, our hands, our shoulders. I seemed to be living in a world parallel to hers, where everything we did together was fraught with particular meaning. And she seemed to know almost nothing about it, to have only the most vague, distant, scarcely focused sense that we together were her future, if only she would wake up and choose what we were living.

I knew I was capable of making up almost anything. But this? Could we be sitting here, shivering, at the edge of the world, huddled together against the darkness, our hands clasped together, our knees touching, staring at each other as if waiting to be told what to do next, if I were making it all up?

"When I was living in Israel, before I came back to marry Max, I fell in love with a woman."

She looked at me calmly, waiting for me to go on.

"It didn't turn out well. But it gave me the sense there was something to know about women and myself in relation to women, something I would one day have to find out and live further."

"Yes," she responded, "I have had thoughts of that kind myself. She was married ? She loved you, but . . ."

"She loved me." I hesitated. "Yes, Sena definitely loved me."

"And still it did not turn out well," she said reflectively.

"It ended violently. Her husband tried to kill me."

"You have lived through something like that? So, you too have been lost, you too have had your obsessions. Is that why you don't believe in mine?"

"I don't believe in anything that holds us back when we're being drawn forward, when the direction has been made clear and all that is left is to say yes to it, to follow it."

"I see," she said, with that maddening lightness that told me, because I knew her well by now, that she was slipping away again. She knew what I was getting at and preferred to avoid it. "Interesting. A very fascinating theory. Please go on. You must tell me more."

But I couldn't say anything more directly, not then. I couldn't say I do not believe in your obsession because I know you have fallen in love with me and nothing but this obsession stands between us. I couldn't say Hadamar, wake up, would you be sitting here with me if our relationship didn't mean a great deal to you? I could say nothing she herself was not already willing to put into words. I couldn't put my arms around her, press her close to me, whisper, kiss her awake, although my body seemed to know exactly how to perform these gestures, seemed even to understand how necessary they were and how much she wanted them, whether or not she would acknowledge the desire.

I was silent as we walked back to the car, wondering if this conversation had brought our relationship as far as it could go and had therefore brought it to an end.

Would I hear from her tomorrow? Would she come by to take a walk with me? And if she did, would it be because she would have forgotten how we had spent the evening, what had been said, how she had fed me, leaned against me, taken my hands, told me her secrets in the mist and darkness, grabbed my arm to squeeze it confidingly as we walked back to the car?

When we got to my house I leaned over to kiss her good-bye. She put her arms around my shoulders. "Now I know what you've been through. I saw it in your eyes when you talked about the woman in Israel."

"That was a long time ago."

"I hate to think of you like that. It scares me for you, it breaks my heart. But you're all right now, aren't you? Tell me you're all right."

"When I'm haunted by the past," I said, because I found her tenderness unspeakably moving, "it is by something from so long ago I'm tempted to say it must have been another life." She smiled, knowingly, as if nothing I said could ever startle or astonish her. And then I felt, once again, as she leaned her head against my shoulder, how much in her own way she showed that she loved me.

"We have, both of us, managed to survive love. That's one of the things we have in common. But once is enough for me. I won't say more than enough. But enough, certainly."

"You've decided never to love again?" I said as easily as I could.

"Never again," she repeated, tweaking me by the nose, as if there were no need for this conversation. "Not at least until I find the one person in the world capable of loving even more than I do."

Was I that person? The boy would have asked. But it was also possible she was marking the boundary of our friendship, trying to tell me where it came to an end. The boy would not have accepted the restriction. I could feel him gathering himself to press her further, to raise his will against hers, but I was held back by a renewed wonder at how many meanings this woman could always manage to jumble together.

I watched her drive off. I heard Max open the door behind me. He had been waiting for me and was relieved that I was home. I too was relieved; his presence drew me out of the misty world in which I drifted about with her, as if we were undersea creatures with only a distant memory of having lived on land.

When she was halfway down the block she leaned far out of the window to wave good-bye. I was as bewildered as ever by what we meant or might have meant or still might come to mean. If only I put aside hesitation and could act? Should the boy take her by storm? Or should I move slowly, as a woman would, with patience, waiting for her to find her own awakening?

12

Max and I never explained the end of our relationship to each other. We never had to. During our last few months we looked at each other as if we were strangers who had met in silence from the windows of trains already slowly moving out of a station in opposite directions. If he loved me as much as he had once loved me, he would have called out, wouldn't he? He would have pulled the window down, run to the door, run after me across the station. He seemed so lonely in his resignation, his willingness to let me go off again, as if I were just going away for a time to be without him.

He had told me, before I had left for Israel, that our lives ran parallel for a stretch, then parted, to come back together farther on. They reminded him of the Merritt Parkway in Connecticut, where he had grown up, the two branches joining to pass through a tunnel, then separating to run on side by side again. He seemed to be certain he could never lose me, except to myself. I don't think he imagined the crossing I was making.

Even my body had started changing. Over that summer it

began to grow lean and muscular but also lighter, as if I had shed some burdened relation to the earth, some weighty obligation to nature and seasons.

I found those months of silent courtship, when she seemed to know, then to forget, suddenly recognize, then evade the passionate interest we had in each other, terrible in their ambiguity. Our language became doubled, divided within itself. We spoke; she heard the clear ring of the apparent meanings, I listened to the implications and reverberations. Her intimate gestures—reaching for my hand, stroking my hair out of my eyes—must have struck her as entirely spontaneous. She would never have wondered about their meaning, while to me they seemed surreptitious revelations of desire.

For my part, my interest in her became more concentrated: what she meant or might have meant, how she managed to veer off, what she knew or guessed or refused to know. I was afraid to lose Hadamar before she had been won; I was afraid to win her and then lose her because she was not ready for the choice she had made. A woman's hesitation. In dreams, I glimpsed her on street corners in foreign cities; I ran after her, lost her again. She came out of a small shop with a bag on her arm, paused beneath the light, glanced at me, and vanished. She was walking along the canals in Amsterdam with a small dog. I followed her; she entered a tall building; a light came on in an upstairs room; I stood beneath the street lamp, waiting.

These were the memory traces of encounters between us in earlier lives. A boy's sense of things. She was intended for me, by temperament and brilliance, sensitivity and beauty, the one woman who had shaped my destiny for hundreds of years. I had only to persevere, governing the despair, the certainty that it would all come to nothing, that she would elude me forever.

There were times, wandering around the house late at night, when I seemed exalted by this askesis, as if I were being put through a lover's trial, transformed through tests of endurance and fidelity, proving myself worthy, acquiring, through my renunciations of desire, a perfect mastery of the self through which, ultimately, I would deserve her. Meanwhile, my body continued to change through the exercise of small, unthinking gestures, subtle enough to pass notice, potent enough to establish roles.

When two women approach a door, who steps back to let the other pass through first? It was always I. Who holds the door, who drives the car, who offers the arm, who jumps up first over the slippery rock, then reaches back to offer a hand to the other? Who is leaned against most? On whose shoulder does crying take place? Who is the stalwart comforter?

A sense of privilege began to inhabit my whole body, which no longer set out into the world in apology for itself, shoulders stooped, breasts submerged, belly sucked in. These transformations gave me a feeling of rightness about myself. I seemed to stride, ready to hunger; my body had acquired arrogance, a pride of limb, an inclination toward self-assertion. I was achieving the mysterious solitude of a boy's body, a physical being that thrives on its own sensations. I was returning to a time when I had been the champion tetherball player at my junior high school, the best batter on our neighborhood baseball team, had gotten suspended from school for climbing a tree and jumping down recklessly when the principal told me to descend slowly. It was a pleasure in movement purely for its own sake, a sense of commanding evenly balanced mental and physical forces, of moving without encumbrance from the wish to the act, innocent of any reason to inhibit impulse. I was becoming the boy she wanted me to be; I was being prepared to become her lover.

Meanwhile, as a woman, I went on brooding, foresaw paradox.

Perhaps Hadamar wanted me as a boy because then she would know perfectly well how to escape me?

13

You are half the size you used to be," Aunt Edith said as we walked into her house. She took me by the chin and looked at me severely, then frowned at Hadamar. "Do you watch out for her? This is no way to cherish a friend. I thought you would know better."

Hadamar looked at me appraisingly, as if she hadn't seen me for a long time.

"Are you really thinner than you were? I honestly hadn't noticed." She took the old woman's hand and kissed it, rather fiercely. "So, give us something to eat," she said, pulling her aunt into the kitchen. "This time I'll keep an eye on you, Kim Chernin," she called back over her shoulder with the same severe expression—playful, threatening, full of the arrogance of a new love that hasn't confessed itself.

That day I ate potatoes with sour cream, an omelet with osetra caviar, although I could hardly eat and had to force myself, because Hadamar and Aunt Edith, who ate well, kept heaping up my plate with extra servings. We had tiny cups of sweet black coffee spiced with cardamom. I was made to eat two pieces of raisin strudel, and then Hadamar took off, the way she often did after an hour or two, to leave me alone, this time with Aunt Edith.

The old woman walked with me into the garden. She cultivated old roses but had a few varieties that hadn't been known at the turn of the century. These intruders, which thrive in the cold Berkeley summers, lived in seclusion in a corner of the garden near an overgrown trellised archway with a wooden swing. It was toward this old-fashioned structure that we were making our way through the twilight.

"The garden needs work," she confided. "It can never get enough attention, roses are like that. They are more fascinating than other flowers, but one has to wonder, sometimes, if they are worth the trouble."

"I don't garden. I've never had a green thumb."

"So I have heard. And yet you do sometimes give the impression you have spent your whole life in a garden. No one has seen much of you lately. Our friends ask about you. You've broken quite a few old hearts, I can tell you."

She was clipping and pinching as we strolled, distractedly, as if she had something in mind she could not decide whether to tell me.

"Roses with too many petals," she sighed, "they never thrive in our summers. It can't get hot enough for them, they can't mature. They wither before they reach their potential. I have found, much to my own distress, that it is best to avoid any rose with more than thirty petals. But those of course are the roses one loves best."

"The garden is filled with white roses," I observed politely.

"White roses love our weather. They want to mature slowly, unworried by the danger that an intense heat will blight them."

"I have a feeling that we're not only talking about roses."

But Aunt Edith had slipped away into one of her silences. Silently then we meandered through the magnificent, overgrown garden, with its stone bridge, weeping birches, trellised figs. We met terra-cotta birdbaths around the turning of a path, eccentric birdhouses hanging from the fruit trees. She cultivated lavender; thyme grew promiscuously over its beds. The early evening was already turning cold, the way it does here in summer.

I was indifferent to these particulars because I had not yet learned to love gardens. I was too busy risking my home, security, a devoted man's passionate love, my own passionate history with him, for a woman who might soon throw me over and break my heart. This, I knew, is what Edith, with her discourse on roses, was trying to tell me.

But she was wrong; I never doubted that she was wrong. She was from an old world, a burdened, pessimistic generation that couldn't afford to imagine the transformative powers of erotic love between women. Even she, who knew everything there was to know, who could never be shocked or taken by surprise, would have been intrigued, I was sure, by my recent experiments. But would she believe me if I told her I was caught between two fundamental organizations of myself, was sometimes made over into a boy, then had to retrieve myself as a woman?

These thoughts, with their troubling intimations, must have alarmed my friend, who returned abruptly out of her reverie to slip her arm through mine. "Hadi is perhaps not so good for you," she said, as if making up her mind to get down to business. "I wanted her to meet you for her sake. She never stops running, as you have seen. I thought you would be good for her. She was a wild, temperamental child, passionate, musical, the most gifted we had seen in a family of gifted children. And where is all that now? Many people admire my niece. She is accomplished, she plays a role in the community. But I know, even if no one else knows, how she spends her nights without sleep. Does she tell you about him, the beloved husband?" She broke off abruptly. "Forgive me if I am betraying a confidence. But is it confidential if no word of it has ever been spoken?"

We had reached the pergola. Edith sat down heavily on the old swing while I stood next to her, holding her basket of white roses.

"He calls her every now and then," I said, eager to continue the conversation. "I've seen her looking nervously at the telephone. Perhaps she imagines he'll come back if she does nothing, leads the same busy life, doesn't go after him, finds nothing else to take his place. Maybe that's what she wants me to be, the one who doesn't really take his place, so the way for him is still open."

The old woman was looking over into the neighbor's garden, where a hummingbird was trying its luck in the pine tree.

"She's not good for you," she repeated, without turning her head. "Nothing means anything to her. You fascinate and amuse her, she'll entertain herself with you, but it's no good, she'll only distract you. You have work to do. Don't run about with Hadi and do nothing."

I loved her in that moment because she was such a fierce old woman. She put her hand decidedly on my arm. "Stick with that lovely husband of yours," she said. "I know what I'm saying." But I had the impression she had said it all before, to someone else who also would not listen.

"It's too late," I declared, although I couldn't get her to look at me. "He and I are the past, we're over."

She tried to laugh, perhaps at a fatalism old people find ridiculous. The sound was mirthless and dry, more like coughing or bitterness.

"Hadamar is your future? That's what you believe? My child, she has never made an unconventional decision in her whole life. I know her all her life, believe me. Would she be where she is now if she had been capable of what you offer?"

"I wasn't capable of it before either," I said reflectively, as I set down the basket of roses.

"You compare yourself to Hadamar? You to Hadamar? After what you've been through?"

I didn't wonder how she knew what I'd been through. Some old women are like that. They know things they shouldn't know, and which no one has ever told them.

I shrugged my shoulders, driving my hands deep into my pockets. I intended to say it lightly. "That's all nothing compared to what I'm going through now." In the narrowing dark it managed to sound melodramatic.

"Don't expect us to feel sorry for you. You know exactly what you are up to. The only mistake you will make is to underestimate the power of conventionality. You wander about in your dreamworld as if it were your own backyard. You go looking for yourself in the past as if the past could explain people like you. The past cannot explain you; you don't belong to the past anymore than you belong to my old garden. You are an odd, fresh sort of being, and if there are other women like you they are right here, hidden from you still, but all around you, next door, down the street . . ."

"Why shouldn't Hadamar come with me then? If I have to go look for them why shouldn't Hadamar come?"

"Hadamar will never go."

"You all underestimate Hadamar. You love her but you diminish her. What sort of love is that?"

"Old love. It has been around for a long time and has nothing more to hope."

"Hadamar is capable of magnificent surrenders. I know that about her if no one else does."

Edith was about to slip off into one of her solitudes, but instead she leaned over to put her head against my hand. "Against a passion like yours," she conceded, "there is no disputing."

"It's not a question of hope. I count entirely on the past. Hadamar is mine because she has always been mine and—"

"One never knows when to take you seriously. But I take you seriously enough to warn you." Again the brittle laugh. "And seriously enough to know you will pay no attention."

14

Hadamar and I are walking down Market Street. She has stopped to look in the window of the navy surplus store. She wants to buy canteens for the little girls, who are off to camp in a few days. I always go with her on these errands, to carry packages, drive the car, open doors, order in restaurants, although she insists on paying the bill and leaves big tips.

I seem to be growing younger with every day, while she is becoming my older woman. She pretends to know nothing of this but does nothing to prevent it. Max and I are always at her house for our Sabbath meal. We know everyone now, know the whole ritual of songs and blessings. Max expects to sit next to Aunt Edith, I expect to jump up at the end of the meal to ask Hadamar to dance. But Aunt Edith no longer seems happy there.

"She thinks I'm ruining you," Hadamar says confidingly as she walks slowly around a rack of regulation navy shirts, her eyes narrowed. "I told her you'd manage to care for yourself."

"I won't, you know. I won't manage. I'll go under."

"Take this," she says, slipping the shirt over my head. She

pushes and prods me to the mirror. With my short hair and blue jeans, and especially now that I am so thin, I remind her, she says, of her father and his brother as little boys, dressed up in sailor suits for family pictures.

"How extraordinary," she exclaims, as if she had never seen me before. "You don't look one bit like yourself, you look like . . . you remind me—" She breaks off in confusion with a dazed, faraway look. "The recognition is so . . . I can't describe it. The familiarity is . . . What is it you remind me of?" She takes a few steps back, her face somber. "I knew you," she whispers. "I've seen you before. Like that. Exactly like that . . ."

I glance at myself in the mirror. No longer a little boy in a sailor suit. A tall young man in a cadet's uniform. There he is, fully visible! And he seems poignantly familiar to me, too, as if I have finally met up with myself. Hadamar looks puzzled, then furious, then outraged, then deeply confused. She is too well bred to point or let her mouth hang open. She draws herself up, draws in her chin, tries to catch her breath, catches a glimpse of herself in the mirror, her pinched face, her pallor.

The cadet is not what I had imagined for myself. A deep melancholy, an undefinable sadness mar his features. He has deep-set eyes with long lashes. It seems a mistake to have dressed him up in a military uniform. He should be sitting by himself, under a linden tree, writing poetry. Why him? I want to have been a young fellow who drank a bottle of vodka sitting on a window ledge, gambled all night, was irresistible to women. I can't imagine this guy jumping to his feet, jumping up onto a table, stomping wildly across shattering glasses.

"This," Hadamar says as she comes very close to me, "this is what you are trying to get me to understand? What is it you want of me? But I want no part of it, do you understand me? I want nothing to do with it."

She must have caught the expression on my face, perhaps as hurt and bewildered as her own.

"No, forgive me," she murmurs. "But just for a moment . . ." She shakes her head, then flicks her hand impatiently. "It's quite maddening, all this nonsense you're always spewing. For a moment I thought . . . as if it were all . . . what we call the past, divided from us, you know, by the thinnest wall, so transparent, almost gossamer."

She looks at me, then through me, then suddenly beyond me, as if she's watching her own world disintegrate. "I see," she concedes. "Is that what it means? Am I, am I in . . ."

One more word and she will be awake. One more word and she, too, will know what I have known for months. We grope along the edge of an attachment that will now either shatter or —right here, in the surplus store on Market Street, between the used shirts and the bell-bottom trousers—confess itself.

There is silence, suspension, the imperceptible rocking and tearing of something about to be said, and then suddenly the whole thing is all too familiar. I know where it is going and how it will end and I have no idea how to make it different. The cadet has vanished. Good riddance. Who needs him? I'm already a better man than he is. The mirror holds two women in a moment of crucial ambiguity, one of them pressing forward, the other in retreat.

They say it's all much easier now. But that's how it was back then, and I imagine there are still places where it's big news that the friendship you have felt for your closest friend may also be, if you care to see it that way, a highly passionate love that would unsettle your life, the way loving me would have turned Hadamar inside out and she didn't want that.

"My god, how hot it is in here. Am I?" she says, somewhat impatiently. "Am I what?"

Glass shatters like that, ice breaks up after a long winter, a stone when it is struck along its fault line and the most poignant communion between women break in the same way, and only someone who is very wide awake will be able to hold on to what has just been about to happen.

Perhaps, I tell myself, because I'm furious at her, perhaps what I feel at moments like this, perhaps what I'm trying to learn by loving this woman is how to come back again and again to this withdrawal, to engage her, watch her slip away, without myself ever losing heart, because I know all this will one day, on both our parts, come to something, to the desire to sustain this desire, to join ourselves through it. Maybe that's what the melancholy cadet has come to teach me.

It's hot, the shirt is heavy, I hate wool, but Hadamar frowns when I try to take it off, pulls the price tag roughly from the sleeve, and walks off to pay for it at the counter.

For her this is a last-minute rescue from knowledge. For me it is her confession of love.

15

The sailor shirt, or something like it, is there in every love affair. Whatever the object, it immediately comes to mean more than it's supposed to mean. Its appearance marks a distinct stage in the progression of intimacy. Why do ordinary objects acquire mysterious powers? To prove that no life need be mundane, nothing is as fixed and static as we have been led to believe. If we are daring or fanciful enough, we can make use of an old shirt to move in and out of the present, change shape, reveal our true intentions while simultaneously keeping them hidden. We can even, if we choose, profess eternal devotion through the breaking of conventional dress codes by wearing a used sailor shirt bought in a surplus store on Market Street.

I wore the sailor shirt regularly to our Sabbath gatherings, with wide-legged corduroy pants. That's the way I said to Max, Hadamar, Aunt Edith, Edgar Rosenwasser, and anyone else present that I was determined to arrange myself as a brazen boy as often as possible. I had given the matter a great deal of thought. I thought women probably got more pleasure from love. But pursuit was a male prerogative not to be lightly dismissed. I was fascinated by the persistent, stealthy devotion of the hunter, but how would it compare to self-surrender?

This guy, the one I was becoming, was the most observant person I had ever encountered; he never gave up, never rested, had fixed his entire capacity for concentration on a cunning, intelligent, obsessive erotic quest. No pleasure, no conceivable fulfillment would ever compare to the enjoyment he derived from watching, following, waiting upon, imagining, plotting, planning his course. The other, whoever she was, the one pursued, would have to take up the entire burden of handing herself over; this guy would never know release, satisfaction, sensual fulfillment. The bird, grasped, would soon be dead in his hand. The erotic ground he crossed was pursuit and capture; in their name he was capable of a melancholy that might have passed for tenderness.

Strange then that my life, not Hadamar's, changed as we became intimate. She saw me before her day began, after it was over, between other arrangements, or she took me with her. I was practically never at home now, although when I came home late and got into bed with Max, he put his arms around me, as if we had agreed that when we were both older, and all this was past, we would still be friends. And that has happened, that is precisely what has happened between us.

I told Max about that time when I had jumped down from the

tree after the principal had told me to come down slowly. It was the sort of thing Max himself would have done, and we laughed about it. I knew how to go from one organization of myself into another, I told him; I knew how to slip easily across borders. As a girl I wore dresses, had long hair, put flowers in my braids, polished my shoes, and liked to wear clean white socks with the cuffs carefully folded. I also liked to get into fights, and one day I punched out the bully in our neighborhood and pinned him to the ground and made him say he was sorry for calling Earle, who lived down the street, a nigger.

What had I done with this border-crossing skill?

Max thought girls had an easier time with these self-arrangements. He thought the sexual identity of a boy got fixed at an earlier age and after that there was no room for choice.

Because these conversations remained abstract, were carried on in a rather lofty tone, I'm not sure Max knew I was talking about my own life and what was happening in it. Sometimes I thought I should grab his hand, pull him down next to me on the couch, look him deep in the eyes, and say, Max, why do you think I am wearing this sailor shirt in the middle of summer?

I never did.

Stevens, during his last visit, had given Hadamar an authenticated page of the first sketch in Beethoven's notebook for the Waldstein Sonata. She'd had it beautifully framed and hung it in the dark-paneled room where her nieces and nephews played string quartets on the first Sundays of every month. No one ever got Hadamar to sing, not even Max when he asked her. She had a real liking for him and always tried to get me to do something to save the marriage. I told her about the strangers at the train windows and she agreed, she'd seen something of that between Max and me but didn't understand it.

Usually, I stayed on after everyone else had gone. Hadamar would feed me leftovers while I was washing the dishes. We could have left the dishes for the housekeeper, who was always there early in the mornings, but I had begun to love washing dishes. When I had not seen Hadamar for several hours, I would think about her pressed up close to me, chattering as she took a wet dish from my hand. One night she drew a soap mustache above my lip, her breast touched my shoulder, our hands met across their shared labor in a lingering, half-noticed, oddly enticing sensuality that hinted at the possibilities of a shared domestic life. I shopped with Hadamar, picked up homemade bread, went walking through Chinatown looking for smoked tea duck, set innumerable long Sabbath tables. We even liked to polish silver together.

There was the window seat in her large room upstairs where we liked to sit because of the view. I suppose we would have gone on like that for a long while if I had been content to leave it there, where holding someone's hand, putting your arm around them doesn't count as a profession of love. Where walking arm in arm, staying up most of the night talking, running together early in the morning still isn't love, because these are two women and women do this sort of thing without committing themselves, even if they are both subtlely reorganized in the process and one of them has grown so thin she can get into her daughter's leftover teenage jeans.

I went out with Hadamar on one particular Saturday night in black velvet pants, a lace shirt, and a black silk vest, strangely elegant for me, but Hadamar was delighted. "My Cherubino," she cried out, offering me her arm as we went down the steps on the way to that opera I never managed to hear or see. I disappeared into the role of Mozart's little page, the transgressive boy who will be allowed to serenade the women or be dressed up as a girl or sent off to the army, whichever proves most convenient, while the important story unfolds elsewhere. So what! Did I care? The edge of her taffeta skirt brushed against my knee whenever she leaned forward. I had her captive beside me, so close I could match my breath to hers or contemplate the dark pulse flowing between us, as her hand rested, casually, indifferently, on my arm.

This woman had the power to make me into anything she wanted me to be. I had the power to be revised as often as she wished to revise me, without ever losing sight of my fundamental pursuit. As wild boy, as page, as melancholy cadet, I would possess her. I had come upon the mysterious calculus of male desire. Wanting her gives me the right to have her, because I want her. Because I desire her, she is mine. And this precisely is how I know myself as male, through this rooted persuasion of privilege in desire.

16

If you close your eyes in the late afternoon, count backward from a hundred, as if walking downstairs from a great height, you start seeing things. They might be street scenes, rooms of great old houses, little parks that had been torn down before you were born. Sometimes the seeing is even more vivid because it's accompanied by sensual impressions or even by feelings. Whole scenes play out before your eyes but not as if you were dreaming. It is easy to make too much of these things, to regard them as evidence that you have lived before, and equally easy to underrate them.

When I told Hadamar about them she would stop whatever she was doing. If we were running in the woods she would stop dead in her tracks, stand close in front of me, and listen. Then we were in my world, sealed off from the meetings and restaurants and exhibits and shopping, from her good manners and social poise and stylized verbal ease. She seemed so much at home, I never realized how much fascination I must have exercised to keep her beside me, her dark eyes fixed on mine as if she were closely considering the merit of what I was saying.

It was this Hadamar I loved, this organization of herself, her powers concentrated, the diffuse, far-flung energy gathered in, held ready. I loved her for my own capacity to make her my embodied dream. I wouldn't have loved her as much if she'd already been what I was determined to see in her. I had penetrated beyond the social disguise, I knew her in some innermost dark secret sanctuary of the self of which she herself was almost ignorant. She came into my memories as if discovering a world she knew well but had long forgotten; she spoke slowly, with a confessional, groping speech, making her way through heavy underbrush, along the overgrown pathways of her childhood, where that wild, tempestuous, gifted girl, who had been abandoned for reasons unknown to me, waited to be taken up again. This was an odd way, perhaps, to court a woman, but that's how I did it at that time. I told her about an old lady sitting by the window with her canary, a thick pair of cataract spectacles on her nose. Hadamar recognized her at once from family stories, the sister of Hadamar's grandmother. But no one had told me these stories.

I used to see a park, or perhaps a large garden, with lawns and delicate tables and chairs scattered among flower beds before a low white building with long windows. There is that very young man in a cadet uniform standing next to a bench, talking earnestly with a woman who can't bring herself to look at him. I like him better now that I can see what a passionate fellow he is. He has acquired color and seems to have filled out some. Maybe he had recently been ill the last time I saw him. When he turns to look over his shoulder, he looks straight at me, his female future. I am penetrated to the core by the piercing expression of his pale blue eyes. This guy runs another kind of risk than the reckless boy I had imagined. He has broken with his family because of this woman.

Oh yes, the whole story is there in his eyes: the elective poverty, the capacity for suffering, the sensitivity to obscure inner states, the nervous vitality, the high-strung intensity. But why am I running into him now? To remind myself not to love the way he must have loved? Hopelessly, for the sake of the trans-formative suffering?

When I described the garden to Hadamar, she recognized it at once from a watercolor painting made by her grandmother's sister, soon after she and her family had moved to Vienna. I could never have seen the park with my own eyes. It had been cleared from the Schottenbastei some time during the 1860s to make room for the Burgtheater, as Edgar Rosenwasser explained to us. And I certainly had never seen the faded aquarelle Hadamar dragged out from a family album of drawings and paintings that went back several generations. But there it was, matching up perfectly with the memories I had of a place that had vanished nearly a century before I was born.

Did I think I had been that tragic young man who had loved the sister of Hadamar's grandmother? Did Hadamar think I had been that young man? Did she believe the obscure, restless, mysterious connection between us could be explained by brief encounters at the theater, long walks through darkening streets to an obscure park, letters written but never answered generations before? Edgar Rosenwasser knew all about the cadet, although he and Aunt Edith debated one late evening whether the fellow had died young of consumption or had committed suicide.

I felt sure it was suicide, but Hadamar turned on me angrily when I offered this opinion, pushed her glass nervously aside, and said harshly, "You cannot distinguish memories from dreams from old stories from the most common reality. If you go on like this you'll end up mad and probably drag the rest of us along with you."

"Hadi, Hadi," Aunt Edith reproached her, "a little confusion about realities wouldn't do you a bit of harm."

"You shouldn't encourage her," Hadamar answered promptly, perhaps uncertain how seriously to say what she was saying. "You don't know what she makes of these things. Ask her, go ahead and ask her. She thinks she was there, she thinks she knows these things from her own memories. I used to think she was fooling around, but now I know better."

Edgar Rosenwasser poured a glass of rosé into a pretty little goblet and pushed it closer to Hadamar. "A person like Kim we understood better in my time," he assured her. "She does not find it necessary to make certain distinctions we ordinary mortals insist upon making. And she is right, she is quite right, I assure you. As you grow old you find that these distinctions do nothing but get on your nerves."

Hadamar was really angry now. "It's dangerous. It's dangerous for her and she's a danger to the rest of us."

"Sit down, Hadamar," Aunt Edith said, and Hadamar sat, obediently. "Kim is our guest. The rest of us seem able to take lightly a matter that has become disturbing only to you. I insist that you apologize."

Hadamar shook her head, put her elbows on the table, and glared at me from between her fists.

"You must apologize," I insisted.

She gave me a really violent stare, as if warning me to take her side or else.

"Yes, she's right," I said reflectively. "I do think I was there, I think these are my own memories, I was that young man who committed suicide, and I'll do it again if Hadamar does not apologize."

Aunt Edith clapped her hands. Edgar Rosenwasser stood up to salute me. I was happier than I'd ever been before in my life. I had made my confession, Hadamar had received it. And now she laughed, at first reluctantly and then with that sudden abandon that made her so irresistibly beautiful.

"Dear guest," she said contritely, with her hands over her heart. "You will not become mad. And I refuse to have you commit suicide."

"Don't let her off," Aunt Edith said, "not so lightly."

"Well, what shall I do to make it up?" Hadamar cried out. "I'll do anything. Ask me anything."

Aunt Edith and Edgar exchanged a meaningful look. "Don't you dare," Hadamar said to them with that passionate, girlish intensity she could take on whenever she pleased. "I won't do it and you know it. You are not to tell her what to ask for, and she is not to guess. Do you hear me, Kim Chernin? Don't even try, because even for you, I won't do it."

"Even for me? You won't do it? Even to keep me from jumping off the bridge?"

Aunt Edith was staring at me. She drummed the table with her fingers, egging me on.

"Stop that, cut it out," Hadamar said to her sharply, as if the game had just turned serious.

Edgar Rosenwasser pushed back his chair.

"Where are you going?" she demanded.

"You know where he's going," I assured her, while Aunt Edith sent me an encouraging, crooked smile. But I had no idea where he was going or what they were playing at.

Hadamar jumped up, ran across the room, threw herself in front of the door. Edgar tried to get past her by tickling her under the chin. I saw them as they must have been many years ago, when she was a girl. But she wouldn't let him get through.

Aunt Edith beckoned to me. "This way," she whispered when I came close. She led me through a small pantry behind the kitchen, through the wide, dark hall, into the music room. Aunt Edith turned on the wall lights, which threw an old, shadowy warmth along the border of the Caucasian rug. Edgar, with Hadamar close behind him, burst into the room.

Aunt Edith pushed me into a chair. She stood behind me as Edgar opened the old, highly polished Bösendorfer, played a few notes, nodded with satisfaction. It was, of course, in perfect tune.

But Hadamar had gone over to the window. She stood silently with her back to us. For everyone else it might have seemed a game, but I thought she was frightened and troubled. I was about to call the whole thing off when Aunt Edith whispered, "We blame it on him, we blame it all on the husband. He used to say to her, If you can't do something perfectly, why do it at all? He imagined he had discovered a flaw in her voice. And since then, since long before she left him and came back from Europe, since even before they were married, she has not been willing to sing. Not even for Edgar, not even for me."

When I got over to the window, Hadamar was gripping the brocade curtain with both hands, staring out into the street. The music room was suspended motionless in the darkness, a luminous Aunt Edith leaning on the back of the chair.

Hadamar said, "They think I will do it for you, if you ask me, because I love you so much. And they are right, I would do it if you insisted."

"Nonsense, it's totally ridiculous. I'd never ask you to do anything you didn't want to do. I didn't even know what was going on. You were all playing; I played along."

"They have been trying to get me to sing again for years. They are subtle, of course, they don't nag, no one pesters me, but I see them waiting, hoping, letting me know it would mean so much to them."

"But you have made up your mind? You are never going to sing again?"

"My own singing irritates me. It isn't, it has never been what I would wish it to be. They blame it on Stevens, and certainly he was very critical, very harsh. But he was right. With so much perfection already in the world, why bother with something less than the best?"

"Are you kidding? Why bother to sing? But why should your singing come in for critical scrutiny of any kind, his or yours? Is that what you do when you begin to sing, you hand yourself over to judgment?"

"They say I could have had a career."

"Well, and if?"

"Stevens didn't think so."

"No career? Therefore never sing again? And who was Stevens to know so much? Who was he?"

"Unerring in his judgment. No matter what."

"But no one is unerring in judgment. Hadamar." I took her by the arm to turn her toward me. She turned away. "It's not possible, it couldn't be tolerated if you gave up singing because of one man's judgment. Really, I mean it, I couldn't stand it."

Now she looked at me. "How you say that. As if it mattered as much as that."

"Well, it has begun to matter a great deal, to me."

"But you would never ask me?"

"Never, if you preferred me not to."

She squeezed my hand, started to say something, changed her mind.

"But I have, you know, already heard you sing. When we were in the woods, in Tilden."

"I wasn't sure you noticed. You never said a word."

"I had the impression I'd better not."

"One word and I would have stopped singing."

"Well, I'm silent now, too. Wordless. Speechless."

"You're on my side?" she said in a low voice.

"Whatever that means, whatever you want it to mean."

We had a long way to go, through all those years of dread and self-doubt and hesitation. She held my hand as we walked back into the room. She dropped me off at my chair, cast a sharp, angry, reproachful look at Aunt Edith, and went to stand behind Edgar Rosenwasser at the piano. She put her hand heavily on his shoulder. Then they fumbled with the scores in a secluded intimacy of their own, shuffling, opening, thumbing through pages, whispering preferences and refusals.

Aunt Edith gripped me by both shoulders with her fierce little hands. "*Ja, ja,*" she whispered, "you have done it, you have made the impossible happen. For you she will do it, after all these years of silence, she will sing for you. Look, look at her, only look."

Edith was struggling hard not to cry; it pursed her lips, brought in more deeply the lines around her eyes, made her look old, used up, and tragic. "*Du hast sie gerettet, sicher, sicher,*" she insisted. "You have saved her. And I, in all my old bitterness, I was certain such a thing was not possible. If you can do this, what can you not accomplish? Look, look at her," she insisted, more urgently this time, because she didn't want me to see her crying. "For so long I haven't seen her like this. For how long? How long since she has been composed, concentrated, like herself? Like my Hadamar?"

17

She had played the piano and violin until she was fifteen years old, when Edgar had heard her sing for the first time. He discovered a true contralto, a dark voice with a warm, expressive timbre. He had taught her at home, as he had been taught by his father before he'd given up singing to pursue his legal studies. He had taught her skillfully, with a stern, loving perseverance that had seen her through the adolescent rebellion against the hours of practice, the demanding, tedious exercises, while preserving the voice's natural beauty.

She had met Stevens the summer after she graduated from Juilliard, with well-placed admirers who expected to help her in her career. Certainly she was good. Perhaps even very good. But was she more than that—one of a kind, unique? Stevens did not think so. The flaw he thought he had discovered in her voice, other people might have heard as a distinctive, troubling beauty. He had demonstrated this flaw so convincingly that she still needed an extraordinary courage to stand quietly in Aunt Edith's music room, preparing to sing to the three people who most loved and understood her.

Hadamar was very pale, her eyes unnaturally large. She tried out a note under her breath. Then, tentatively, in a half voice, she moved uneasily up and down the scale, through a comfortable range of two octaves. It was soon clear that her voice was not out of practice. The tone was full and round, the pitch exact. But how was this possible? Had she struck a compromise with herself, never to sing again in public or to sing music she loved for her own pleasure, only to practice exercises and scales, secretly, so that the voice wouldn't lose its agility and focus? If this was true, what a strange penance she had imposed upon herself for an imagined imperfection. And how like Hadamar to yield so completely to Stevens' judgment while holding on to some unextinguished core belief in herself.

A sequence of notes reaching toward high A, a touch of roughness in the voice. She looked stricken, backed away from the keyboard, glanced anxiously around the room, as if to assure herself that Stevens was not present.

Edgar played through the passage again, brought her up an octave. Her voice wavered, he changed keys, she followed him, the note held.

It was a dark voice, richer than I had imagined when I'd heard her in the woods, an arresting voice, agile, fluid, expressive. Edgar was working his way through what must have been their familiar repertoire. A couple of short Brahms songs, a Bach aria, a few simple seventeenth-century airs, which she treated as vocal exercises. Edgar was evidently trying to keep the whole thing casual, but now and again he would glance at Aunt Edith with an expression of such urgent tenderness, with so much hope and apprehension that the old woman would grip me fiercely by the shoulders, while Hadamar, in a remote, uneasy communion with her own voice, shared Edgar's expression of anguished dread.

Hadamar and I had listened often to these songs; we had heard them late into the night, sung by Maureen Forrester and Kathleen Ferrier, her favorite singers. We had discussed their technique, listened over and over to particular passages. She had taught me more than I had learned during my cave years of obsessive listening. Because she had been planning to sing for me? Because she wanted to teach me how to appreciate her voice?

Edgar toyed casually with a melody from Mahler's "*Das Lied von der Erde*." Hadamar stood quietly as he played through a piano version he must have worked out for her many years before. He looked at her questioningly. If she sang, her voice would have to provide the moody, disturbing sound cluster that should have been rendered by woodwinds and horns.

> *Herbstnebel wallen bläulich überm See*
> *Von Reif bezogen stehen alle Gräser;*

Man meint, ein Künstler habe Staub von Jade
Uber die feinen Blüten ausgestreut.

Her face was perfectly calm, almost transparent, as the beautiful timbre filled the room with an impression of dark sobbing, although her delivery was still restrained. I was seeing her for the first time uncluttered by all her partial evasions and hesitations. Pride, haughtiness, her always slightly strained high spirits, the polished, somewhat artificial gestures had all given way to a perfect simplicity. She was standing next to Edgar now, her face slightly averted, her hands folded on the edge of the piano.

Mein Herz ist müde, Meine kleine Lampe
Erlosch mit Knistern, es gemahnt mich an den Schlaf
Sonne der Liebe, willst du nie mehr scheinen,
Um meine bitter'n Tränen milde auszutrocknen?

The word *Schlaf* (sleep) seemed to detach itself, float out into the room and hover there, as if to provide a space large enough to rest in, before it was allowed to die away.

It wasn't a large voice, but it had an intense, penetrating quality that made it difficult to hold back tears. If Stevens had found it flawed, it couldn't have been because of that slight, anguishing edge that brightened the voice and made it seem, in a sequence of high notes, discontinuous with its own darkness. It could only have been because he couldn't tolerate its emotional power and therefore had willfully destroyed her belief in it.

I could have killed him for that.

She stood silently when the song came to an end, and then she slowly, heavily let her chin sink to her chest. Unaccompanied, she repeated the last two lines of the song, as if she had, at last, found a way to stand aside to let the words pass through her.

The singular gesture with which she had cast herself off transfigured her. She was lit now by a deep glow, as if she were shining through herself. Knowable, fully revealed, graspable for the first time — this is who she was, there would be no way to draw closer to her or know her better. That's what our courtship had been about, this revelation of warmth at the heart of her coolness and disengagement.

There are moments in every love affair when the love crystallizes, is more pure than it will ever be again. I wanted to give my self, my whole life, my entire capacity to love so that I could save Hadamar, from him, for me, and for herself. Was that what I was here for? Was that what I had been trying to do? Was that what loving her meant for me?

Toscanini wasn't lightly given to enthusiasms. But when Rosa Ponselle, the most beautiful voice of her age, came back to greet him after a performance, he threw himself on his knees before her. Is that what a man could do because he had no fear that the gesture would debase him?

I remembered Father Zosima, the way he had knelt down before Dmitri Karamazov to acknowledge his suffering. And Stravinsky, on his return to Russia after the years of exile, making one of those low bows of homage that sweep the earth, gestures through which spiritual authority and expressive power are declared.

I got to my feet and stood hesitating in front of my chair as Hadamar finished the song. But she walked straight toward me, without a word, stood in front of me, lifted her chin with a wild, jubilant expression, and grabbed hold of my hands. Could I? Down on my knees? She looked at me defiantly, as if she had been preparing me for this. So much revelation, risk, daring, self-exposure on her part. And I could not throw myself down on my knees to celebrate that?

I heard Edith cry out softly, my name or Hadamar's, perhaps in approval or warning, a severe note, as if we had all somehow gone too far.

"*Ja, ja,*" Edgar said encouragingly to me. "*Wir beide, knien,* both of us, yes, down on our knees." He moved slowly, stiffly, with a grim smile of self-reproach, as if he were remembering something that should never have been forgotten.

It was, I suppose, one of those characteristic Bonheim family jokes. They used to give me the feeling we had embarked on some old ritual, something rehearsed and traditional, although they arose spontaneously and were carried out with a keen sense of improvisation and complicity.

"*Und du?*" Hadamar said in high humor. "What about you?"

Down on my knees to acknowledge the gift Hadamar had once given up for Stevens? Head bowed to witness how much she was still capable of achieving? Was she waiting for me to risk as much as she had risked, to give myself as completely?

Cross this line, something in the atmosphere seemed to say. Go so far you can never turn back. They were playing at whatever they were playing, while I had reached the edge to which my own history was driving me.

And so I did it—yes, just like that, I crossed definitively out of the female version of myself into a breathtaking reorganization. I had decided to live my life as a boy. That was how it came about, in Aunt Edith's music room, down on my knees, in the year 1978, on a cold night in late summer.

Part 3

18

And so began my life as a boy.

To begin with, this dramatic change gave rise to serious contemplation about the nature of the self. But these meditations were no longer carried on in my cavelike study, or during sleepless nights wandering about the house. I now slept soundly and snored, woke up at dawn, pulled on my hiking boots, and was off into the hills. Up there, it was said, one could encounter mountain lions out on the prowl for the deer who came down to water themselves in the meadow pools. The sign near the parking lot gave precise instructions about these potential encounters. One should never turn one's back and run in fear. Mountain lions should be approached directly; you should wave your arms and make as much noise as possible.

Yes!

In the parking lot there was a composite drawing of a man who had raped several women on the lonely hiking trails up in the hills. Many women now went running in twos or threes, and most women I knew refused to go up into the hills alone even in broad daylight. I myself preferred the thought of the mountain lion to a meeting with that man, but he no longer kept me out of the woods when I wanted to be there.

Up in the hills I ran and walked fast and climbed a low tree to watch the sun rise, but I was busy with my thoughts. It seemed to me that we humans were free to choose the shape of ourselves, if only we could get back far enough into our dark beginnings, before identities had been thrust upon us. During my long years in the cave, I must have been wandering about in those primordial self-swamps. I could now see how easy it would have been to get lost there. That was why my daughter, who had sensed these dangers, took pains to draw me out of myself when she came home from school. That is why Max had been so devoted and attentive, knowing himself to be the marker of the way back.

It was now clear to me that the self could be rearranged, like the mosaics of a kaleidoscope. I could be anything in the world I suffered myself to be; this boy was only the beginning! I needed a boy's reckless, devil-may-care spirit so that I could break definitively with the past. Self-reproach, a sensitivity to the needs of others, a pained awareness of the suffering I was causing Max had to be cast aside. I needed ruthlessness, a conviction about the rightness of going my own way. I needed a restless momentum that nothing could contain. I needed a boy's imperative thrust into the future, a force of becoming that couldn't be held back by any tempered consideration.

A boy doesn't last for long. He's a stormy, transitional figure, fired up with impatience for a world that is his to conquer. Girls (as I knew them) moved with docility into their future, aware of impending limitation, nostalgic for the greater freedoms of the past. A woman down on her knees, subservient, humiliated, bowed to the authority of a superior power—that's what kneeling down had meant for women. But my first fully chosen act as a boy had brought me to my knees. What did this mean?

Perhaps I had found in Hadamar the lost, despairing woman who needed to be saved, so that I could free myself from being that woman. If so, the gesture of homage concealed a terrific pleasure that I had escaped from her condition, which I professed to worship but secretly despised. Or could the deep-rooted nature of male pride be expressed only through a gesture that willingly shrugged it off?

These were serious matters, deserving serious consideration. Because of them, I found myself, whenever Hadamar was busy, hanging out in the avenue cafés, studying the girls and young women who walked by. I had the impression that the whole scene, everything I surveyed—undergraduates and street people, craftsmen, pedestrians, dope dealers, stray dogs, street musicians—had been put there for my pleasure.

Was this the world from which I had closed myself off through all those years, the world in which I as a woman had moved stealthily, like a deer at the end of the hunting season?

Now I saw it unabashedly as mine, there for me to conquer and claim, a vast carnival of possibilities spread out for my consumption. The innocence and arrogance of this, perhaps because I was a new boy and still remembered my former timidity, took my breath away. It did not seem possible that this was the same world in which, I had always believed, I would have gone under without the protection of a man. What had I feared, what had I dreaded? Why had I been so certain I couldn't survive this world, which gazed back at me so seductively now, waiting for me to thrust myself out into it and stake my claim?

To reflect more closely on these matters I cultivated a café with several outdoor tables. I sat with my legs stretched out, my hands behind my head, and observed the scene complacently. I was surprised to find that many women returned my glances, as if my indelicate curiosity intrigued them.

The girls and women who strolled by were a different kind of creature than I had beheld before. They seemed to move in their own unique terrain, filled with secrets and whispered unknowns. It was strange, intoxicating to perceive them now as other than me, mysterious, my opposite, yet oddly inclined to me. What I thought of them mattered to them. I interested them in a way I had never imagined. If this is what it was like to be a boy, why had I waited so long, why hadn't I tried it out sooner?

I jumped up, tossed my cigarette into the street, and went after an undergraduate who was loaded down with books. She didn't seem the least bit startled when I offered to help carry them. She handed over a hefty bundle, and we had a nice time sauntering down Telegraph Avenue, until I began to feel disloyal to Hadamar, deposited the books on the Dwinelle steps, and ran back to finish my coffee.

Was it arrogance, this peculiar sense that I would be liked because I took for granted that I would be? It wasn't a question of looks. I looked okay in tight pants and my sailor shirt. I had a tan that year and let my short hair curl over my ears and down my neck. People had always told me I had a great smile, so now I was grinning a lot. I must have had a rogue's look in my eyes because I was up to mischief and I felt, no shit, I'm a boy, I'm irresistible.

I probably would have turned into a cool, callous fellow, full of self-conceit, if it hadn't been for Hadamar and for the yearning that brought me out of my house late at night to run all over the neighborhood. So that I could pass by her house and perhaps run into her? Forget that!

When I was seventeen, staying with my family in Europe, my boy cousin used to climb out of his second story window every night, climb across the roof, lower himself down into my window on the other side of the house, and get into bed with me. Sometimes he arrived soaking wet and we had to wrap him in blankets before he could stop shivering and make love. Late in the night, still wary of disturbing his parents, he would take to the roof again and climb out over the steep gables to drop silently back into his own bed.

I now began to dream about ladders, which were, it seemed, essential to a boy's identity. Ladders led to a high virginal chamber, a promised bride, a secluded princess, a girl locked up by her guardian. Sometimes the ladders led unceremoniously, through great hazard and momentous consequence, to forbidden nights of love. Well, why not? I was certainly capable of climbing over the Bonheim garden fence, fetching the ladder out of the shed, making my way to Hadamar's room. Was this behavior outrageous or simply new and untried? The confusion about such things may be one of the reasons women don't usually decide to become boys.

In October we had two full moons. By the time the second moon showed up I couldn't sleep, I couldn't stay in bed, I couldn't get the idea of ladders out of my head. I wanted Hadamar and I went out to get her.

Since I had cast off everything vulnerable, secret, soft still open in myself, these very traits had attached me more than ever to Hadamar, the woman who had held on to them. It was an extraordinary erotic calculus. The more I established myself as a boy, the greater grew both my contempt for women and my desire. Hadamar had now become everything I no longer wished to be. Therefore, I had won my place beneath Hadamar's window. Because I am a boy it is my perfect right to enter her room, make my way through the darkness, turn the cover back, lay her naked before me. She cannot protest; she has invited this, by being what I no longer am. My hand will reach out to take in the luxury of her, a seamless caress to the damp beginning of things. To gain entrance here has become my purpose. She must concede my claim, smooth arms slipping around me, head tipped back, eyes half closed, torso arched toward me. If I kneel between her legs it is not now because I am down on my knees to witness and worship. This time it will be a serious act of repossession.

I got over the fence, jumped down, crouched behind the elm tree, ran over to the shed, inched the door open, dragged the ladder across the lawn. But then I started laughing, because I was a new boy without much practice. Hadamar caught sight of me and ran down into the garden, kissed me on both cheeks, and told me to go home and get to bed.

I was beginning to think boys had it pretty good; whatever they did, they couldn't go far wrong so long as they behaved like boys. "Go on, go," she said, pushing me toward the gate. And then suddenly I was furious. Didn't she know I had become a boy? Didn't she know all this was serious?

19

A Friday has come round again and has grown late. Max and I have been walking home from Hadamar's house. She has walked with us part of the way in silence, as far from me as possible, on the other side of Max. There are times when she is so close to me I know that if I reach out my hand hers will already have moved to take it. But tonight she has consistently refused to look at me. Endlessly, during dinner, she has fussed with the little girls, who stood up on their chairs and made oinking noises. Hadamar is hesitating, reconsidering the path we have been cutting together. This makes me desperate, then furious, and I do not say good-bye to her when she turns back to walk home alone.

A beautiful Labrador comes down the steps of the grand house up the street from ours. He walks along with us, keeping close to Max, who scratches the dog's head thoughtfully. Max has borrowed a motorcycle from a friend. He has been taking off by himself for long weekends, with a sleeping bag and a small tent. But tonight we are suddenly, unexpectedly in a mood we'll come to know well many years later, when we have understood how much good we did for each other by being together until we didn't need to be together anymore.

"Do you remember the time we camped out in the delta and you got covered with mosquito bites?" he asks nostalgically, drawing my arm through his.

"Are you taking off for the weekend?"

"You've seemed tense again lately. Is it Hadamar? I thought you might like to come along."

"What do you think of her? Is she worth going through whatever one would have to go through for her?"

"Edith thinks she wants you to give her back what she herself gave up a long time ago. But what's in it for you?"

"Edith talks to you about Hadamar?"

"She says things more or less to herself. I'm not sure I'm meant to overhear them."

"You are certainly meant to hear them. She's trying to get you to wake up, to fight for me."

We've walked down past our house, past the rose garden, on down to Rose Walk, where the steps curve inward toward each other from opposite sides of the stone bench, where two tall rose-bushes have been planted. I've been walking along on the stone bench, from one bush to the other, then turning sharply and walking back, as if I'm on sentry duty. Max has been walking along with me as I pace. He's worried about me and isn't sure if he should let me know.

"When you first came back from Israel," he says tentatively, taking my hand to pull me down from the bench, "when I first came for you in Scotland, you used to say that you could have gone on being friends with Sena if only you had gone on being only friends."

He was forcing himself to say what he felt he must, for my sake and because he would try to hold on to me, even though he was ready to let me go. "You've never spoken of Sena since, not one word. But if you're looking for Sena in Hadamar, you will lose Hadamar, too. It seems to me it would be better for you to remember Sena. To think about her again, talk about her to someone. You can talk to me. I'm not afraid of anything you want to tell me."

We had made our way up the curving steps to the wide stone landing from which another flight of stairs opened into the terraced gardens. The houses rising on both sides were dark and shuttered, except for a light in a downstairs window farther along the lane. Max clenched his hands, pressed them together, as if he knew it would do no good to say these things to me. I would only resent them.

"Of course my friendship with Hadamar is not like Sena," I answered impatiently. I almost never thought about Sena. I had willfully forgotten her, except as a fact, empty, without meaning, incapable of reaching the emotion in which the story of Sena was held.

He seemed suddenly very happy, as if he had taken my answer for a reassurance that I was not in love with Hadamar. But I had meant that Hadamar was not like Sena because Hadamar had not grown up on a kibbutz, was not afraid of the world outside, would not lose her nerve in the last minute. She was not like Sena, because with Hadamar I had a future.

He bundled me in his arms that way he did. I was sitting in front of him on a lower step; he put his chin on my head. I remembered what it was like to slip away from myself, lean on him, let whatever power I had and all desire cross over between us and return to me from him, while I took on any yielding, any surrender he might have felt and gave it back to him, but slyly, safely held by me as if it were my own.

I stood up and came to sit next to him, shoulder to shoulder, companionably.

"There's something about your personality," he went on, weighing his words carefully. But there was no need for that. We were old chums meeting up after a long separation, brothers or teammates who had once been very close.

"You probably won't like what I'm going to say," he said in an easier tone. Perhaps he too had felt how much we were comrades now, discussing a woman with whom one of us was in love. "You transform the people you love, your personality puts a kind of pressure on them and changes them, actually changes them. So, in a way, you never encounter them. You encounter what

you've made them become. It's very flattering. What you pro-
duce really is a better version of oneself. But it makes people
very uneasy. They are afraid any day now they'll fall back into
being a more commonplace self and disappoint you."

"But you've gone through all this and managed to find a way
to live with me. Are you saying not many people could?"

"It hasn't been easy."

"No," I said, moving away from him and getting to my feet. "It
hasn't been easy. Not for you and not for me, either."

This seemed to surprise him. His surprise irritated me. He
seemed so comfortable in the assumption that I had been the difficult one over the years.

"I know life hasn't been easy for you," he conceded. "That's
what has made life difficult for me."

"And no one else would be able to handle it? Is that what
you're saying?" I had made up my mind not to cry and not to raise
my voice either.

A light came on in the window of the second story of the
house closest to us. He got up, drew me by the arm. We walked
farther along the path, past the sheltered roses in their wire
cages.

I managed to keep my voice low. "So I'd better stay with you
because when you come right down to it no one else would be
able to stand me?"

"Is that what I'm saying?"

"That's what it amounts to, although of course the real message is very well disguised."

"I see what's going wrong between you and Hadamar."

"You know what's going on but I don't?"

"Hadamar is afraid of you. I never met Sena, but I'm sure she was afraid, too."

"But you, of course, are not."

He looked around nervously, as if he knew we were into one of those scenes. My voice had risen perceptibly. "No, I'm not," he said, "not anymore, I'm no longer afraid."

"It sounds like a very heroic self-conquest," I said, forcing my voice down in a thankless effort. "Therefore, since you're the only person in the world who could put up with me, I guess I'd better stick with you?"

"Well, if you left me for Hadamar you'd be leaving me to be alone."

"You're absolutely sure of that? You know Hadamar better than I do? You know what she's really like, what she's capable of deciding? And how did you arrive at this special knowledge that eludes me?"

"Women like Hadamar—"

"She's become a category?" I said violently.

"Women like Hadamar choose safety first. Everything else comes after."

I was walking away from him fast, farther up the path, to the steps that open out between the last houses of the lane into Hawthorne Terrace. He was keeping up with me, but I turned suddenly to face him. "Perhaps she feels safer with me in the way I know her than she's ever felt before."

"Like Sena?"

It was I who grabbed him by the arm. We stood close together, but I was, it seemed to me, standing up on the bench looking down at him. "What do you know about Sena? You know nothing but what I've told you. The only Sena you know has come through me. But there you stand, Mr. Self-satisfied, you know all about women like Hadamar, you know all about Sena. You know what there is to know about me. It seems that the only knowledge you lack is of yourself. Do you know why, do you have any idea why you are so kindly, so considerately offering these great insights to me?"

"I remember how it was when I came for you in Scotland."

"And I remember you. Your triumph, your pleasure in my despair. The savior you got to play and how much you liked it."

He pushed me aside and walked back down the lane, past the rosebushes, past the dark houses in which here and there lights were coming on in upstairs windows, but I did not run after him.

"The only mistake I made back then," I said, loudly enough, "was calling you when I should have gone on and seen it through myself, whatever it cost me. That's what I should have done. That's what I'll do this time."

He had almost reached the street. But that got to him. "So far as I know you don't have a penny of your own and no way to earn a living."

"You've actually said that? Good, I'll remember it."

We were standing in front of each other again, although I never took a step toward him. "You've managed to say I can't make it on my own, no one else could put up with me, I wouldn't be able to make a living, I would scare off anyone who loved me, and of course, of course, sooner or later I'll fall apart."

"Those are your fears, not mine." He had lowered his tone but his voice was shaking.

"Oh, that's good. And nothing you say is designed to set off these fears? You're simply observing the nature of things? Calmly, philosophically. And I, of course, I'm imagining hidden meanings, disturbing messages in what you say. And if that's so, what does that make me?"

"Upset. Unhappy. Almost as unhappy as I've ever seen you."

"And you of course are waiting to comfort me. But you never do see the role you play in bringing me to this state."

I remembered what it had been like to burrow down in him for comfort, the way he must have imagined I would do now, sooner or later, as if I could still slip back over to that other less comradely side, the place where I had always been with this man, who had always comforted me.

But what state was I in? He was worried about me, I was

upset, he was protective and annoying, I was irritated with him—and all this merely from habit. We had said these things before, and now we had said them again. The repetition was the release we'd been waiting for. We were shaken and relieved and had been brought forward, as if we had finally had this conversation once too many times and could no longer believe in it.

In the silence, he smiled, I grinned back at him, we both shrugged.

"Well," he said, "I guess that's that."

"I guess it is," I answered, and we were brought back out into our comradeship, because there was really nothing we could do about where our relationship had now been carried. Since the night of Hadamar's little recital, I had glided from one bank of a great river to the other. Now I was here with Max. We were standing a bit oddly together on the same shore, never in some ways more alike. Over there, across the way, on the shore from which I had come, was Hadamar. The condition of my having her seemed to be the far-flung erotic distance I had put between us. I might spend my life trying to cross back to where she was, where I had already been with her, when it had only been thought of as friendship.

A small wind was scuffling along through the caged roses, breaking up the overheated air. When it passed, the finality of where he and I had come out together weighed heavily on us.

"I don't see how you can stand that sailor shirt," he said, because he had known for years how much I hated heat.

He was almost always, at any time of day or night, a sweet, kind, and tender man. But he had depths, shadows, darkness like anyone else; perhaps in him they were even more dangerous because it was so hard to believe in them. Before now, when we disagreed, no matter how loudly I said what I had to say, I always thought he was right, no matter how vehemently I stood up for myself.

He and I sat on the upper steps of Rose Walk, at the final station of this conversation we'd had so many times and now would not have ever again. We put our elbows on our knees, brooding over the choice we weren't really making. We sat in that night heat unbroken by shadow, caught up in a strange competition, not for Hadamar, but Max and me in a rivalry for the organization of myself. I would not take off my shirt. It was Hadamar's pledge to me, binding, beyond all rational calculation.

20

I am making coffee in the small espresso pot early one morning after we returned from our walk. She is upstairs taking a bath. I get two cups, carry them into the room with the French doors, sit down to wait for her. The time has come; I have known it since she called this morning. It will be our day of confrontation, challenge, rupture or resolution. I have no idea how it will come about. Will I say something? Is she ready to say something to me?

The room is charged with the tension of what is to come. Light hurls itself from the glass surfaces of etchings and drawings. When Hadamar comes in she'll shut the door that seals us off from the rest of the house. But for now, the little girls come racing in after their dog and charge out through the French doors, which slam shut behind them, setting on edge the delicate nerves of the glass lamp. An elderly man peeps in, smiles politely, disappointed that Hadamar is not there; he retreats quietly. I can hear stirring and bustle upstairs in the guests' part of the house, but I have no idea who's there, for how long they have come, or what events are planned for them.

What happens in this room today may change the customs of this house, close its doors, transform its public nature. Hadamar comes into the room in a pale blue kimono, her hair wet, her feet bare, dragging the telephone by a long cord. The languorous femininity makes me aware, with pride, of my own sharp lines, bony knees in running shorts, hard, flat stomach with no folds, arms ready to fell a forest of trees to reach the woman I desire. She finishes her conversation and sets the phone down on the floor next to us. "I brought you a few things to look over," she says, in the light voice that means she has something serious to say. "Close the door, would you?" she asks, laying out a few drawings on the floor. This seems significant to me. Before now she has always closed the door herself.

"Look at this," she says, when I crouch behind her. She hands a cup of coffee to me over her shoulder, picks up hers, sips it reflectively. "Do you recognize him?"

It's a pen and ink drawing of an old man, a masterful execution of bold, elegant lines, delicate brushstrokes that draw out the bittersweet humor that puckers his lips, the serious, somber expression in his half-closed eyes.

"Of course, Edgar," I say, leaning over Hadamar's shoulder, "but how very strange it also is. Somehow, in this portrait of an aging man, one seems to glimpse the whole world he comes from. Here is this man we know so well, this dear face that is so familiar to us, and yet at the same time, there's the whole troubled epoch through which he lived. Do you see it that way? Do you agree?"

"I doubt whether everyone would see it quite like that. What you say is, of course, very complimentary to the artist." I have my arms around her because of the odd way we're sitting. She has handed me another drawing without turning to face me. It's a faded pastel; I'm holding it in front of her, leaning in to take a better look. "Aunt Edith? Aunt Edith as a young woman? But surely not the same artist. The style is so different, so, I don't know, soft, flattering, almost sentimental."

"You don't care for it?"

"Not much at all. The likeness must be good; I can still make it out after all these years. But how eager the artist has been to remove any trace of her sharpness, her cunning. Yet I would think these traits must have been there when she was young and that the artist, instead of revealing them, thinks it's his job to hide them."

"You love Aunt Edith very much? You believe in her? You would do what she advises you to do?" She has placed both drawings down on the floor, covering the third, which I have only glimpsed.

"Would I take her advice? Maybe; it depends on what it was. If I wanted to do it, I would surely listen to her."

"Aunt Edith thinks that you're in love with me. She advises me to let myself fall in love with you."

"Aunt Edith advises you to fall in love—"

"No, don't," Hadamar says when I try to get up. "Stay where you are. I have something to show you." She reaches for the third drawing, removes it carefully from the pile.

"But if Aunt Edith advises you to fall in love, that means she knows you are not . . . or not yet already in love?"

"Aunt Edith doesn't think very highly of me, you know. She thinks I'm far too conventional to fall in love with a woman . . . even if I have already . . . fallen in love."

"I see." I try to get to my feet. "You have already fallen in love."

"No, don't move," she says. "Stay put. Did you know your voice was shaking? Stay where you are. It's hard enough to say what I'm trying to say. I couldn't manage if I had to look at you."

I stand up, I have to stand up, I'm towering over her.

"You really like that drawing of Edgar Rosenwasser? You really think it's better than the pastel? But the pastel, you know, was made by a very famous Berlin artist, a friend of the family. And the drawing of Edgar was made . . . did you know? Did you guess? Were you only trying to flatter me? It was made by me . . ."

The door has swung open into the garden. I blame my shivering on the early morning cold that penetrates the room.

"I showed this drawing to Stevens before we were married," she says, with that smothered mortification I hear in her voice whenever she mentions him. "He put it aside without saying a word. I have no idea whether he liked it or despised it. He seemed completely indifferent to it. Yes, completely indifferent, although of course he knew that I had made it."

"Hadamar," I said, crouching down to put my arms around her. "Listen here. If only you would let me—"

"But don't you see?" she said, leaning back against me. "That's exactly the problem. If I were to change my whole life, turn everything inside out, would it be myself I was finding? Or would I become what you want me to be, what you have made of me because you love me?"

"I'm not striking a bargain, I'm just loving you the way I do. I see what I see in you. How can I help that? To me, you are . . . simply . . ."

She stood up fast with her back to me, took a few steps, stopped in the middle of the room. "Don't say it. I don't want you to put a name to me, not one word, not one phrase, no definition."

"What did Stevens think you were?"

"Less than I thought I was before I met him. Much less than I am beginning to think I am now that I know you."

I had acquired the authority to make her think of herself more highly. I had changed the way she felt about herself. Therefore, she could lose herself to me the way she had been lost in him?

She had needed me to have an arrogance equal to his own, a similar pride of self-regard, an authority that could challenge and depose his. Had I accomplished this so successfully that I had come to be what he had been, to pose the same danger of appropriating her? Her words had been lightly spoken, sharply delivered. But it was so like Hadamar, this turning back while moving forward, this revocation of what was being simultaneously given. Only Hadamar could have contrived this impasse, and only I perhaps could have fallen for it.

I stood up and took a few steps toward the door, yes I did, without a word. It was a boy's cunning. It brought her over to me. That was all I had to do, that was it. I had to be able to leave, and I could never lose her. She stood beside me, shoulder to shoulder, and slipped her arm around my waist. "I know what I've been doing to you. I know what you've been going through. But you know I love you. You've always known. You've seen through every feint. I've never been able to fool you or mislead you. I've counted on that. You've known me better than anyone ever has, and therefore you know how dangerous you are to me."

"Dangerous? To you?"

"The one who knows best. Can you deny it? The one who names me before I name myself. Tell me the truth, can you deny it?"

"I could, yes, I could deny it, but the whole thing makes me furious, it's so absurd. Because I know you, because I have seen you clearly and love what I have seen, I'm a danger to you and have already lost you before we've begun to figure out—"

"If I were already what you imagine, if I were just a small part of what you see or even of what I become when I'm with you . . ."

"You sound amazingly like Max. Has he talked to you about me? Is this a conspiracy?"

"I've been coming to this understanding myself. I reached it before Max and I ever had a conversation about you. He merely confirms what I already know."

"But you've spoken to him about me?"

"Not as you imagine. Certainly not as you imagine. These are my own fears, my own hesitations, my own doubts about myself."

"So you won't take Aunt Edith's advice? You are, after all, too conventional to love . . . what you love?"

"Look at me, don't walk out of here, we have to face each other. Nothing has been decided."

"I can't make my way through all this, Hadamar. I'm lost in words that seem to mean one thing then turn out to mean another. I'm lost in the endless contradiction. It seems to me you've just told me a decision has been made. That you have made it."

"I've only been trying to say that I'm afraid."

"And therefore?"

"I need time . . ."

"Time? But we have all the time in the world. Who's rushing?"

"I thought you needed to know. You're leaving Max for me. But what if I . . . what if I'm not ready . . ."

"Max and I are leaving each other because we are ready to let each other go."

"So I'm free?" She said it lightly, with an almost inaudible calculation. "I've made no promise to you? You expect nothing?"

"I expect everything. What I wish for, believe in, am willing to risk is entirely a matter for me. You have nothing to say about it. You don't even have to know."

"I have a feeling you always win arguments."

"I always do."

"So there, you see," she said, triumphantly, with her mischievous smile. "You see why I'm so afraid of you?"

21

From far off I catch the rumor of my other life. Max has found a house in the extended neighborhood, on a hill street near the park. He has packed only his personal belongings. What is to happen later with our house, the furnishings of many years, the paintings given to us by artist friends, our collection of records, will be decided later. One day when I had gone home to fetch my bike, I had heard from upstairs that frightened, angry sobbing of a man who almost never cries and resents that he's been driven to it. I closed the door quietly and hurried into my study, knowing it would be dangerous if I ran to him upstairs, where we would think our grief, this sorrow at an ending, meant we should stay together. But I had moved on; I had Hadamar.

Every love affair has a few days of this kind, when all you wish is that you will be allowed to go on, with everything pending, promised. Nothing has been decided. Everything is known. It's a question of hanging out while things get ready. All it takes is perfect faith, a capacity to let things ripen slowly. A faith of this kind doesn't come easily to women; it is carried by a benign arrogance, a serene self-regard that believes you deserve to have things turn out the way you want them to. These are qualities I had not possessed before.

The door to the Bonheim mansion had swung itself shut, closing the world out of our virgin solitude. If we slept at all, it was casually downstairs in the music room for a few hours. We reminded me of a brother and sister, twins perhaps, separated during the school year, who were now at home for the winter holidays.

We ate fruit, dried fruit, nuts, and Hediard chocolate. She sang day and night, whisking around the room to find a book or record she wanted me to know, dragging us out into the little patio garden, where there was always something to be weeded or cut back. Eventually she persuaded me to accompany her on the beautiful old spinet with its ornate candle holders. On the night I finally played through the much-repeated Brahm's song without a mistake or hesitation, she lit the candles, turned off the lights, and came to sit next to me. She had a wonderful way, especially when she sang softly, of floating her voice out on her breath and letting it ride there with something of the same poise a bird shows as it gives itself over to the currents of air it has learned to master. When she wasn't singing, we used to sit back to back by the French doors, or at night out on the patio, a single shawl covering both of us, as we went through the history of our attachment, figuring out together what everything must have meant, and when we first knew what we thought we knew or divined or intended.

She knew in retrospect the way she could veer off as she was getting close to me, and now we laughed about it together because she admitted how much it must have made me suffer. She admired me for my patience, the wonderful discretion I had shown, my absolute confidence in her.

I could have sworn there were moments when she wanted me to put my arms around her, hold her against me as tightly as I could, kiss her, make her mine, possess her. She seemed to be asking with the inclination of her head, in the way her hands lightly touched my shoulder, the easy way she would enter into silence with me.

Sometimes, with these gestures, she seemed to speak in a language of lost signs with which I, too, in my time as a woman, had once been familiar. These delicate moves between us seemed endlessly fascinating to her. She was content, sometimes for what seemed hours, to take my hand, lean up against me, lift and drop my fingers. She liked to feel my breath against her cheek. She would gaze at my hands, curiously, as if learning to know them. Sometimes she would put my right hand on her shoulder, against her knee, then lightly, quickly, against her breast. She would grow contemplative, as if quietly absorbing these impressions. This erotic shadow-play, which absorbed and inspired her, seemed only to confuse and frustrate me. Once, not very long ago, I too would have known how to take delight in this game. The boy had lost the key to it, and all enthusiasm for what was slow, repeated, prolonged. For me, sitting next to her, there was the quick rise of desire, the imperative impulse to act. I was set in motion and was instantly impatient with gestures that seemed both invitations and impediments. I was on fire, checked, quenched, heated up again simply because she had turned to look at me and looked away. She liked the way a single glance could bring me across the room. She was full of laughter and secrets and partial revelations, and I was growing angry, sullen, moody, somber, reproachful.

At times she looked at me with surprise, as if she expected from me a delicacy and subtlety equal to her own, a dreamy capacity to drift through slow increments of desire to a consummation that must have seemed inevitable to her, but that I thought she was withholding from me.

We had a game, during which we chased each other back and forth through time, meeting up, catching sight of each other, following, losing the other through our long history of love and separation. I saw us together at the opera in Vienna; she remembered the white cashmere shawl she had been carrying. We met on the Kahlenberg; she remembered the bowl of whipped cream on our table. We took long walks in the Alps, ran across each other in a first-class carriage on the way to Greece. She needed a sleeping compartment; I gave up mine.

I tell Hadamar exactly what it had been like to stand with my arms crossed, leaning against the window in the narrow corridor of the train while she undressed and got into bed a few inches away from me, on the other side of that thin glass barrier covered with a heavy drape, the unknown woman who would rise up languorously the following morning, whom I would help down from the train and never see again.

Now, too, my desire for her grows imperious, seems to seek an absolute mastery over her and her erotic world, by which I am teased and tantalized, drawn on, restrained, excited, held back, so that something cruel, violent, brutal begins to show up in my desire. I have become a boy so that I can know these desires, to want, to demand, to require the giving over, the yielding of the other. It is she who must be undressed, stripped bare, laid open to me. She must be paid back for the ambiguity, the waiting that seems never to come to an end, the promises that lead to further promises that open into endless vistas of desire, a world in which she seems effortlessly at home, while I have begun to feel more and more like a stalker, the stealthy watcher growing close to his prey, ready to leap out and take her.

She arouses something terrible and frightening in me, even beyond this will to possession. This alien growth rises up between us, rancorous, malevolent, vindictive, isolating us from each other, confusing us. The desire that should bring us together has taken a dangerous turn. It can now only drive us apart.

"Stop staring at me," she says one morning, when I look at her over coffee. Her tone suggests she's not to be taken too seriously.

"I am not staring."

"But you're waiting for something," she says, thoughtfully, a faint irritation to her voice. "Waiting. Waiting."

"Of course I'm waiting." The irritation in my voice is more pronounced.

"Why can't you be satisfied with what we have?"

"Like Tantalus, satisfied with his fruit and water?"

"Are you crazy? You think I'm withholding something from you?" She looks outraged, puzzled. "These days haven't been, for you too . . . ? They haven't been . . . ? Well, what have they been, these days we've spent together?"

"Listen here," I said, "now listen here." I couldn't find words for what I wanted to say. My responses came up through my body. Shake her, my body said. Pick her up, carry her over to the couch, be brutal to her. "They have been," I forced myself to say, "of course, wonderful for me, too." But I could have strangled her.

"Then I'd say you have an incredible genius for destroying your own happiness."

Did I? Was it true? No one had ever said anything like that to me before.

"It makes me think no one will ever be able to give you what you want. No matter what you get, it won't be right, something will be missing."

I thought she was going to say *I'll never be enough for you.*

"That's enough," I said, "stop there." I was surprised by the ominous sound in my own voice. She had given herself to me, it was true; she had closed out the world to close us in together. But I felt deprived, cheated, toyed with, tricked. I needed something to grasp, close in my fists, throw my arms around, press to me, intrude into to keep myself from drowning in this subtle sensual stuff in which we had been drifting. For a moment or two, in the sheer unspeakableness of it, I felt capable of anything, any violence, any outrage.

"Don't," she said, leaning across the table to touch my shoulder. "Don't take it so hard. I didn't mean it." And then her voice, coaxing, conciliatory, as if she had been aware of the danger, drew us back from that edge where I had wanted to destroy her.

I took a breath. I smiled, vaguely.

"You're worse than any man I've ever known," she said, but I could tell she meant it playfully.

"I'm only a boy. I have no experience in these things. I'm not used to such tormenting proximity to a beautiful woman."

"How strange you are." She looked at me thoughtfully. "I almost believe you."

But the idea seemed to please her. She held out her hand. "Come here," she said in a large tone of forgiveness. "Tell me how I've made you suffer. Come here, tell me."

Then one afternoon she fell asleep against my shoulder when

we were sitting under the chestnut tree. Suddenly I wanted to kiss her the way a boy wants to kiss the first girl he has ever been close to—reverently, shyly. It even occurred to me that I could kiss her so lightly she wouldn't wake up, but then the kiss wouldn't have been known. That might lead to late-night confession, and that would be good, I thought. As I leaned over to kiss her, I could smell on her breath the dried apricots we had just been eating.

22

I am making coffee in the small espresso pot early one morning. She is upstairs taking a bath. The phone rings, she picks it up from there, I go on making coffee, wondering why she has suddenly answered the phone after all these days when we have pretended not to hear it. How many days? Three, four? Even that many? I get two cups, carry them into the room with the French doors, sit down to wait for her.

Hadamar comes into the room in her pale blue kimono, her hair wet, her feet bare, dragging the telephone by a long cord.

"Are you an editor?" she asks, holding the phone with her shoulder as she draws the dead hortensias from a black vase.

"Maybe, sure, why not, I guess I am."

She has been telling me I have to find paid work if I'm serious about leaving Max. She doesn't see any reason why I would have to leave Max. She has said this with a grave, deep look and put her finger to my lips whenever I have tried to answer. But if I want to leave him, I need work.

"There's someone here looking for an editor. I don't know

her, she's the friend of a friend, she's right there if you want to talk to her."

She says all this with her chin covering the receiver. I shrug; who cares? Aunt Edith has recently introduced me to the only surviving daughter of a playwright once as famous in Vienna as Schnitzler, his contemporary. His poetry has never been translated into English, a task she is willing to assign to me. Hadamar and I have spent several hours translating a lullaby he wrote to his daughter, which I have set to a moody chord progression in a very simple melodic line she has embellished, so that we now have a lullaby between us, if ever we need to sing each other to sleep.

Hadamar hands me the phone. Somehow, during the bath, she has managed to return to the ordinary world, the perfunctory gesture. It must be this transformation that has allowed her to reach out, unthinkingly, to pick up the phone. Already, she seems almost to have forgotten the time we have just lived through together, the promise of its inevitability. She's holding the bouquet of dead flowers in her hand. The woman looking for an editor, this woman Hadamar doesn't know, this friend of a distant friend is the woman from the tree sacrifice. She's the woman who three or four years earlier had put her head on my shoulder and cried. She is Alix Graham, the woman for whom I first became a boy.

The potential in all this will take a while to fall into place. But it will soon turn out that Alix Graham lives in our neighborhood, just as Aunt Edith had imagined such women might. She lives even closer to me than Hadamar, right down Easter Way, then a few feet to the right up Cragmont, then up through the overgrown garden to a cottage you can't see from the street, right along the route on which I run from my house to Hadamar's.

Choices, paths, turning points, crossroads seem to be scattered with an incredible profligacy. Whoever keeps an eye on these things must have a wicked sense of humor and on the whole means well by us, I suppose. But none of this seems apparent as Hadamar bustles about. I hesitate, while she nods her head urgently at me, and so I agree to an appointment to look over the talk Alix Graham is going to give, the following week, at a conference on women's spirituality down the coast in Santa Barbara.

Are you an editor, do you want work, did you happen to be present when Hadamar, for reasons unknown to you, decided to answer the phone? Did you agree to meet the woman at the other end of the line?

Is this an act through which the will shows itself to be free? Or is it a surrender to a pattern that has been prodding you, egging you on over the many generations you seem to have always, at the last minute, waited too long, proved yourself to be too delicate, too conscientious, too worried about the brutality of your own desire? And so you let the moment pass? As you have done now, too?

Or have you?

23

We're going. We'll drive down along the coast to Santa Barbara. We'll borrow the convertible belonging to Edgar Rosenwasser's niece. We'll take rooms in the graduate school sponsoring the conference. There are no single rooms left but Hadamar agrees that we can take a room together. She packs a small bag of clothes, repacks mine because she thinks I have brought too many jeans.

"Don't you have a long skirt or a dress? I seem to remember you dressed very differently when we first met. What happened to those clothes?"

"They're all too large. They don't suit me."

She looks at me appraisingly. "It won't do," she says with a shake of her head. "Look at you, always in shorts, short hair, turning muscular. You wouldn't believe how young you look. And so, so . . . I don't know. They'll think I'm trying to smuggle a boy into the conference."

"I like the way I look. I've been trying to look this way all my life. What's wrong with it?"

We are going to hear lectures, participate in rituals, hear poetry recited, attend an art exhibit, discuss the reemergence of the great goddess among contemporary women. I'm sure no one will know I've turned into a boy. In moments like this, when she's playful and bantering with me, Hadamar rarely means what she says, even when she says things that would be highly perceptive, if only she meant them. But how will I feel in a world of female deities and desires? Does it matter that I, too, was once a woman? Or will I seem alien, duplicitous, deceitful? It would make more sense for us to go anywhere in the world together, but Hadamar will hear of nothing else—no weekend alone in Mendocino, no backpacking trip. If we're going off together, the purpose has to be educational, serious, part of our preparation for a new life. She is full of plans and excitement, has been reading about Janáček's research into Bohemian folk songs, imagines there must be undiscovered women's music of the same type— lullabies, work songs, learning games—slowly getting lost on backcountry roads as the older women die out and no one is left to teach the words to the children. Hadamar wants to find musicians and dancers and researchers; she's convinced we can put together a woman's opera with women of all ages, professionals and amateurs, older women, children. I'm to write the libretto; she will organize the project and, yes, take on the contralto lead.

We drive out through the park to the ocean for something to do, a small excursion, a walk on the beach. We're restless and nervous; we're leaving tomorrow, unless Hadamar changes her mind—again.

We don't get out of the car. We have parked on the divider between two lanes of fast-moving traffic. It has begun to get dark. For some reason, on this occasion, Hadamar has been driving. She grips the wheel nervously. A car comes up fast along the ocean. A shadow grows from Hadamar's shoulders, moves unsteadily, rises across the backseat, then disintegrates. Her face leaps up out of the darkness, moody, withdrawn, brooding, undecided.

The silence is tense, hostile; we're visibly shaken as another car comes by fast. This time, in the speeding light, her eyes are luminous, engaging, full of excitement. "Let's keep talking," she says. "Nothing has been decided; let's talk all night if we have to." Darkness again. Silence. Shadows rise up and fall from her as cars pass us. Darkness returns and she says, "I don't know what you're thinking. Tell me what you're thinking. I can't stand it when you're quiet like that."

Then I'm looking at her mouth, relentlessly shaping its words, her face visible again in the roaring traffic. There are now two faces gliding across her face, as if the upper face, with its warmth and cultivation, grave forehead and expressive eyes, were actively detaching itself from the spoiled, resentful, almost bitter expression her mouth gives to the lower face, that other face I had not noticed before.

"Are you going to say something? Are we going to sit here all night in silence? If it means so much to you, I can go with you."

"Do I have to remind you again? It was you who wanted to go. Your choice, your excitement. It was never my decision," I say roughly. "Why would I want to run off with you to a women's conference?"

This time, in the sudden light, I can see the great fatigue around her mouth, while her eyes seem sunk in an ageless, unappeasable sorrow.

"Everything with you becomes so dramatic," she says, impatiently now. "You're taking a four-hour drive down the coast, but one begins to feel you're taking off forever, launching yourself, setting out into the wild. How could anyone else possibly go with you on such a journey? But if it's not a big deal, only a long weekend near the ocean, what difference does it make if I go or not? You'll go, you'll be back, you'll have stories to tell, I'll be here to listen, nothing will have changed."

"I've created all this drama? If it's only a four-hour drive, and you were excited to begin with, and we're all packed and leaving tomorrow, why did you change your mind? You make light of it, but anyone who looks can see you're afraid."

The fear scatters all over the car, rushing toward me, dying away when it can't pass through the window. Our car shakes violently as a truck rumbles up from behind her, cleaves through darkness, leaves darkness behind.

"I'm afraid? Oh, yes, I'm afraid. I'm not ready for this, not at this time in my life, not now."

"Suddenly you're not ready?"

"Okay, okay, I thought I would be ready but I'm not, not yet, not tomorrow."

"But you will be ready later on? Next year, two years from now? All I have to do is wait and someday we'll drive down the coast together?"

"I can't commit myself," she says harshly, in a cold, cutting voice. "I won't make promises. I told you all along I won't make promises. If you're ready to take off, go."

I start to get out of the car. This boyish act of turning away, cutting her off, being willing to lose her, has become habitual. She puts her hand on my shoulder. I brush her off, open the door, and stand in the cold, windy, whispering night, on the narrow divide between the fast-moving lanes of opposing traffic. I could walk back through the park, I could hitch a ride, but she's standing next to me. She's facing me, pressing up so close to me that to embrace her my arms have only to move of their own accord, opening the way arms do, then closing around her.

"I don't want to lose you," she says, as if it were simply beyond dispute. "But I can't go."

"I see, I see," I whisper back, the gypsy lover who hasn't managed to persuade his lady to leave her stockings of silk and shoes of bright green leather.

"I don't want to lose you," she says again in that low, husky voice that will make you stay with her, on any terms, forever.

"I understand. I believe you. You don't want to lose me."

"But I can't go. I can't. I can't."

So Max was right, except that I was holding her in my arms. He was right, and Edith, too. Most people didn't choose to live at the extremes of themselves or cast themselves into new configurations or start a new life or take off on a great adventure. But here she was in a way they would not easily have imagined, clinging to me, as if I could keep her safe. I had to hide and protect her from the danger I myself posed to her. Her hair was wet, she wouldn't let go of me, the wind was covering us with salt, and we just kept shivering, huddled up together next to the car, neither one of us wearing a jacket, because the day had been warm when we started out from Berkeley and no one here ever learns to believe in the violent changes of the weather, even when you have lived in this wild place for most of your life.

Part 4

24

I did a lot of running around during that conference. Every time I heard something I thought might interest Hadamar, I rushed from the lecture hall, raced to the telephone upstairs in the dorm. I knew she would want to hear about the way contemporary women, who were not part of any organized movement or sisterhood, who had never heard of one another, who were living obscure lives here and there all over the country, were all, during the last decade, painting images of a mother goddess, with her fat belly, her pendulous breasts, her enigmatic smile of consternation and forgiveness. Sometimes the artists had painted roots breaking up through crusted earth, and these, too, they said were paintings of the goddess. No one knew how everyone had rediscovered her at the same time, not the art historian collecting the paintings or the students crowding the historian's lectures, writing letters of appreciation to the artists, whose work I had just seen during an hour-long slide show, after which I went running to call Hadamar, to tell her about this new world emerging in which she could be active, organize things, find her own creative participation.

There were women in long dresses and robes, who smelled of musk and patchouli, wore their hair long, wore bells, earrings, silver bracelets; they wafted and tinkled and rang whenever they moved. I saw others with short hair and muscular legs, but I never found out if they were born-again boys, or had been born that way, or had progressed more smoothly than I into their virility.

I started to leave a long message on Hadamar's phone machine, which cut me off after three minutes, and so I called back and left another message and called back to leave a third, got impatient, and sat down to write her a letter, although I knew I would be back home before the letter arrived.

I heard a lecture on the significance of the Virgin Mary, who was, the historian claimed, through her many representational evolutions and her eventual assumption, a surviving remnant within Christianity of the great goddess of the ancient world. Some of these things would interest Hadamar more than they interested me, so I wrote them down dutifully in this letter that became over the long weekend a record and a diary, full of scholarly details, wild schemes of my own, sudden insights about our friendship. Through it, I proclaimed, these same historic forces had been acting that now, among women generally, on behalf of the entire culture, were unearthing the lost feminine principle, its hermaphroditism, its eros, its seductive priestesses and androgynous boy-girls. The fertile goddess, her roots breaking through dry earth, this emergent, celebratory sense of female power and bonding and transformation had drawn Hadamar and me together, I was sure.

I left quite a few messages that weekend, running back and forth, writing in my notebook, chattering with the women who sat next to me in the various lectures. I also left detailed instructions to the conference in case Hadamar wanted to change her mind and join me. I left her a phone number where I could be reached just before dinner at six o'clock. I became the object of good-natured jesting when several women guessed I was in love and couldn't wait for my lover to show up. They would have been surprised, I thought, to discover how far Hadamar and I still were from the erotic communion they seemed to have found so easily, together.

I heard a lecture that proposed that the medieval women who had been burned as witches were practitioners of the old Neolithic matriarchal religions. They had been midwives, wise women, herbalists, and healers, and with their destruction the old ways of female knowing and bonding had been destroyed. There was a hushed, solemn mood in the lecture hall during this talk; many women huddled together, some cried softly to acknowledge this persecution we all seemed to know intimately, collectively, impersonally.

I heard a talk, which turned out not to be very popular with many of the others, about the son-lover of the goddess in ancient myth. I knew quite a lot about these fertile, amatory couples because Hadamar and I had been reading *The Golden Bough*. Frazer had described the great Mother Goddess, whom he regarded as the personification of the reproductive energies of nature. There was always a young lover associated with her, mortal yet divine, the hero with whom she mated year by year to assist the propagation of plants and animals. I'd been intrigued by this coupling of the older, majestic woman with the ardent, potent boy, but I never had the least idea they had anything to do with erotic love between women, or anything much to do with me.

Many women objected to these myths and stories, which they saw as a patriarchal incursion into an earlier, more exclusive form of female bonding. Some women left the lecture room in protest. The few of us who remained talked about the need for tolerance of divergent points of view. We, however, were at one in our understanding that the boy-lover of these old tales was a representative image for adolescent girls, too. We admired the perfect androgyny of the figure and felt invited, through it, to reclaim virilities and capacities we had given up when forced to become purely feminine girls.

The boys of ancient Crete, as they appeared in murals and on vases, with their reedlike figures, broad shoulders, small hips, long mass of corkscrew curls, were hard to distinguish from the Cretan girls, whose sacred rites included, we learned, a dance with bulls. That virility, leaping across a bull's back, that supreme grace in an athletic act of worship—are those the qualities I, in ancient Crete, would have possessed? Would I have known that lighthearted, sunburnt androgyny that slipped so easily back and forth between genders?

Several women looked at me curiously while this discussion was going on: sizing me up, sending out, I thought, across the clutter of chairs and notebooks, an invitation to act, to cross the room, to strike up a conversation. Why me?

Were there other boys present? It wasn't a question of short hair, muscular thighs; the tinkling, swaying, jingling, sweet-smelling women could have been boys in disguise. You couldn't judge by looks, not even by confessions. There are boys who have no idea they are boys, who live out their lives disguised in a discreet, perfumed femininity, unaware that their true destiny lies in the ability to take a risk, to court perpetual transformation in a ruthless pursuit of the self.

Did the women who gazed at me sense these hard things about me? Were they intrigued by the ruthlessness I might so easily have shown by starting up, while the weekend lasted, a relationship with any one of them, without saying a word about Hadamar? And was I, in my made-over self, now capable of this?

My body was capable; the gaze I returned to the dark-skinned woman with a silver snake ring was capable of any betrayal in the name of adventure. If I had been, for a longer time, a lad who cultivated the sublime egocentricity of erotic experience, I would have seen no reason to look away, to take up my notes, to remind myself, when the dark-skinned woman finally smiled, that I had a letter to write to Hadamar.

I wrote my notes; I bent over my desk and wrote them dutifully; for a single instant before I took them up, I saw myself in the dark woman's gaze as if I had just stepped up to a stark and revealing mirror. I saw myself as I lounged in my seat, my legs stuck out into the aisle, knees spread wide, my head tipped back appraising the scene; I saw my heartfelt arrogance, based, it seemed, on nothing more than my being precisely who I was, in my tanned, thrusting toughness. My posture said, Me, I'm here. I am worthy of your attention.

What a rogue I had become, what a ridiculous scoundrel of a hard boy. And how I loved myself!

After the talk, I met up with Alix Graham, who had organized the conference and given the opening address. She was curious to know what I thought about this business of the goddess with her boy-lovers, which had caused the only disruption during the conference. A few women joined us as we talked. I thought they softened toward the idea of the boy, especially when I came up with other images of androgynous female potency. I mentioned Artemis's nymphs, who hunted with her, ran with her dogs, were the unrivaled powers over woodlands and mountains, virgins all, with muscular thighs. I grew eloquent as I talked about the sinew in the wild, untamed girls, the delicate long curls in the Cretan boys.

One of the women now pointed out that I had misunderstood the meaning of the word "virgin," which had nothing to do with a woman's erotic immaturity, but was instead a word that meant complete unto herself, without a man.

Someone else reminded us of Aura, the wild girl who had been raped by Dionysus. This example, which I'd hoped to avoid, drove the discussion down a new, heated course, in which it was claimed that girls, however muscular, could nevertheless still easily be raped by gods. Others, who knew their mythology better, remembered Apollo's flaying of the boy Marsyas. But we could not agree whether this horror, too, should be regarded as a form of rape.

Later that night I went out dancing at a bar on the edge of town, where the women from our conference danced together. I, who had come without a partner, was asked to dance by several men and didn't refuse, although this put some distance between me and the other women and probably discredited the androgynous ideals I had been promoting earlier in the day.

At the conference, several women had obviously seen me as

a boy. Here, the men saw me as a woman. When the women had looked at me, the virile object of their desire, I had been expected to start things going. The men looked at me because I suggested availability.

The gaze, it seemed, had power over the configuration of the self. I could throw out a boy's challenge to the man's intrusion or welcome the implication of his stare, rocking eerily back and forth between the erotic possibilities of the moment. But when I turned away and asked a woman to dance, there was no doubt about how we addressed each other as partners: her hands on my shoulders, mine on her hips; mine the first step toward her, to which she responded by moving in closer to me, moving right up against me before she stepped back to follow my lead.

I could have this woman; I could take her back to my room, where Hadamar should have been; I could lie with her all night, waking her when she fell asleep because the right to desire is mine. The turbid sweetness that unsettles, the dark wetness that receives—this woman will offer them up to me simply for the taking. This innocent, groping, adolescent hand will close, finally, on her breast. I am a boy who gets what I want because I'm willing to give her the pleasure of my wanting—that, and nothing more. This is apparent when the music stops and she clings to me, without actually touching me, because we both know the first touch has to come from me.

She is nameless; she waits for me to ask for her name, but I don't ask. If I kiss her, here in the darkness behind the jukebox, where the women have been dancing together, if I offer her a cigarette, if I take her hand in mine when she reaches out, will my life break with itself and begin over?

I wonder what will happen when the music starts up again and I don't ask her to dance; when, instead, I look at another woman who's walking toward the bar, trying to catch my eye. Indescribable, this power I feel, this dazed sense of an infinite, transgressive potential. Just now, in this dark and smoky place, with sweet fifties records on the jukebox, the smell of beer and sawdust and her scent of tea roses, this woman tries to read in my eyes the message of her own desirability. If I withhold this tribute she won't turn and walk away even if I stand here while the music starts playing (as I must, because I'm so new to all this and because of Hadamar). She'll step closer to me, she'll put a cigarette in my lips, she'll rest her head on my shoulder because, she believes, these acts will make me want her more. And she's right. In this moment, when I feel her breast against my shoulder, I want nothing in the world but this woman, who wears a tiny silver double axe around her neck, has tied her waist with an intricate strand of handmade rope, so that her long, white caftan shirt swells out over her hips, which are pressed so close to me I can feel the demanding, inexorable pulse of her.

"Its late," I say, because of Hadamar. "We have an early morning session. Will you be there? Will I see you again?"

It seems the chivalrous thing to say, and it lets her down lightly, although she looks back over her shoulder to give me a somber, mocking, curious glance as I leave her at her car.

I see her again on the last day of the conference, in the late afternoon; most of the women have formed a huge circle and are dancing together. Some of the women make loud, baying sounds, a few tear off their shirts and dance with their breasts triumphantly naked. I join in the dancing when the woman from the bar skips by me with naked breasts; I grab her hand, she pulls me into the circle, and I find that I'm standing next to Alix Graham.

"You move fast," Alix shouts to me above the baying and the music. "You've made a conquest," she says, nodding toward the woman on the other side of me. "But I thought you were sweet on me."

Sweet Alix, who had no idea, and never would come to know, even when she knew me so much better, how stunned I was to find these women so available. They were so nonchalant in their erotic play, skipping about large-breasted and bare-breasted, ripe for gathering.

"Hey, honey," Alix says, dancing in front of me to take the woman by the elbow, "I saw her first. I invited her; if she spends the night with someone, it will be with me."

I didn't know how seriously to take their banter. I suppose the whole thing might have gone in whatever direction I wanted to take it. I could have had either one of these women or both, because I had crossed over into a world where traditional taboos were unlikely to be respected. But I was eager to be off. Alix Graham walked me to my car. She leaned in to kiss me good-bye and I didn't see her again until we met at a women's retreat in the Berkeley Hills. I had too much to tell Hadamar. I knew I wouldn't be able to sleep until I saw her again. I had hardly slept for the last three nights. I was constantly getting up to write Hadamar letters because I saw the way for us now, among women like these, to find a life together.

25

Hadamar had news for me, too, when I got back home, although I heard it first from Aunt Edith, who had been waiting for me in the garden, waiting to tell me that Hadamar was seeing Max.

"Hadamar?"

Somewhere else, far from us, I was falling down a flight of stairs, flailing, stumbling, reaching out to support myself, slipping farther.

"Max?"

This falling went on and on, but it didn't concern me. I was trying to figure something out. I knew that these names—Max, Hadamar—should have been familiar.

Aunt Edith put her arm around my shoulders. Therefore, I noticed that I was shaking. Shaking? But I'm a boy, I protested. Boys do not shake when they've been thrown down. If a boy cries, he cries when he's alone. I wasn't crying. A boy feels anger before he feels grief. My left hand was balled up in a fist; I could, for the first time in my life, imagine the hard pleasure of revenge.

"Hadamar has been seeing Max?" My voice, when I spoke, was composed and thoughtful. "When? For how long? Since I left? Since he moved out? Before I left?"

These questions might have been spoken in a shrill voice, or hoarsely shouted. Perhaps I'd spoken them that way? I tore myself out of Edith's embrace, stomped off into the garden, grabbed a branch from the old plum tree and broke it off.

"When? For how long? Since I left? Since he moved out? Before I left?" My voice was calm, although I had just repeated myself. I was about to repeat myself again; I noticed that my voice was rising, and that I was holding the branch of a plum tree in my hand. I knew exactly what those two names meant. Hadamar and Max! The names of the two people who had just betrayed me!

"We live for eighty years," Aunt Edith said, watching the white moth settle on the arm of a garden chair. "A butterfly lives for a single day. But in that day it acquires more wisdom than some of us will get in a lifetime."

I thought that I would be stunned into silence, but instead I was talking very fast.

"Hadamar and Max," I said, as if their names had suddenly become too hot to hold between my lips. "Hadamar and Max," I repeated, ready now to feel devastated but the devastation would not come. "It never once occurred to me. But now that it has come about it seems to be just what one might have expected."

"*Qwatsch,* nonsense," she said, crossing her arms on her chest. "They have taken each other in place of you. *Ja,* good, it is safer like this but it won't last. How could it?"

She was right. It lasted for about three months, and then Max grew tired of it. He had paid me back, I thought, by taking the woman I wanted. But he never knew the woman I loved or he wouldn't have grown tired of her. Whatever triumph he might have had came to nothing. He and I seemed to be in love with the same woman, but we were not. He couldn't know Hadamar as I had known her. No born-man could.

That is what I told Aunt Edith.

"Who could know Hadamar," she responded caustically, "when Hadamar does not yet know herself?"

"But I'm not even upset. Am I really not upset? I should be devastated. Am I devastated? I came home with so much news, so much to tell her, I came home with a whole new life for us. But it's all suddenly so far away, as if it happened to someone else a long time ago. I am no longer the same person who set out to drive down to Santa Barbara on Thursday. Do you know what I mean? I don't seem to care. I'm strangely above it all. It doesn't matter; how is that possible? It doesn't seem to matter at all."

Aunt Edith shook her head. "That will come later, but you'll survive it."

"I'm stunned. Dazed. Really, I am. The whole thing troubles

me, if it troubles me at all, only because I didn't foresee it. But I brought it about. They wouldn't even know each other except for me. What would they have to say to each other? What *do* they say?"

"I imagine they spend much of their time talking about you?"

We leaned our heads together, looked out into the bay, where the fog was stretched beneath a clear, still, cloudless blue sky. I was seeing everything in too much detail, too precisely. That meant trouble was coming. "It all seems to have happened so long ago," I repeated. "Maybe even to have happened so many times before that I must have known it would happen again. But I thought it all meant something else, as if Hadamar . . . as if she were meant for me, belonged to me, could be known and understood only by me."

"And now you find that Hadamar was only your pretext?"

"Pretext? Hadamar, for me? Pretext for what?"

The old woman put a finger against my lips. "Why ask what you already know?"

"A pretext . . ." I really had no idea what she was talking about. "You think I wasn't in love with her?"

"*Ach,* love," she said, as if talking about a companion who had grown stale along the way and had been left behind a long time ago.

"Well, what? What are you trying to say to me? I don't get it."

Had I been courting Hadamar for him? Had I found him a woman to rescue in place of myself? Was I able to leave him because I had left Hadamar to him, left her to take my place as the despairing woman? Had I set off on Thursday knowing what would happen, precisely because I had intended it? But if I had let him step into the part I was supposed to play, how would he play it differently than I did?

"*Ja, ja.*" Aunt Edith nodded her head. "He will be there to save her from herself. As he was there to save you. You maybe would have saved her for herself, but who is to say? Hadamar made decisions a long, long time ago. Perhaps, as you sometimes say, these choices were made generations ago. *Ja,* maybe, it could be, maybe . . ."

She turned to face me with one of those abrupt, imperious gestures of hers. She took my face between her hands, tilted my head up, gazed ruthlessly into my eyes, and shook her head again. "Who brought it about? You? The patterns you believe in? The repetition of lives over many generations? I am too old to bother with questions like these. But this I see. You are precisely where you wanted to be. You wanted Hadamar to be in this new life? You wanted to bring her with you? So good, she wouldn't come, she couldn't come. But does it matter? You don't need anyone to take care of you, you will take any kind of risk. So good. If this has come about through Hadamar, if she has been the means of bringing you to this, well, yes, I suppose that could be called love. Why not?"

"If I didn't know you better I'd say you were a cynical old lady and that you were up to no good."

"Up to no good is certainly true. But cynical? Why bother?"

"So I am where I wanted to be. Where I wanted to be, precisely."

"And maybe already a little bit in love with someone else?"

"*Ach,* love," I said in her own voice, but she didn't smile. "Every decade of my life, love means something different. It has a way of coming on abruptly, seizing me with a terrible urgency and then dropping me again. I seem to have learned this a long time ago . . ."

Now she smiled. "The real lovers do not learn the nature of love. Everyone else, everyone who renounces love or grows tired of it or watches other people get used up by it learns something about love. But the lovers, no, never, they cannot learn. You are one of those, the unteachables. You will go on loving, passionately loving, until you are older even than I am, and you will never be able to figure out what love is for. I hear you already, I hear you debating."

She managed to sound just like me. She raised her voice, she made wide gestures, her eyes looked heated and excited. "Is love the means we use to egg ourselves on into our own transformations? Is it selfish, solipsistic, irrelevant to anyone but the lover? Or is love the root that thrusts us back into the secret workings of the universe?"

She put her hand on my head, as if to keep me from taking it wrong, or perhaps to bless me.

"You see in my future a lot of late nights and early morning conversations?" I was suddenly in the best of spirits.

"But I am one of those," she went on, "who learned a long time ago to get free of love, long before you were born."

"You learned what I am not capable of learning . . ."

"Love is terrible," she said. "Barbarous. Impersonal. It has designs of its own. It makes use of us, of those of us who do not get out of the way."

"But that's what I mean by patterns—"

"A nice word," she interrupted. "A lovely word for something unpredictable and infernal."

"My new friends would say sacred." It was I now who had a chance to laugh.

"Your new friends . . ."

"I've met a woman named Alix Graham. She thinks the strangest thoughts, so much stranger than anything I've come up with on my own. She doesn't believe in love at all, not the kind that makes people into couples. She thinks it's old-fashioned, patriarchal. She says women are separating from men to find themselves again as a tribe, erotic but not romantic, explorers but not of a new world. That's the sort of thing she teaches, about a matriarchal world that we have lost sight of a long time ago."

"A true believer is not for you. You will run through these women one after another, looking for what you will never find. You may even come back to Hadamar, who may in her own way go on waiting for you. Not that it will do either of you a bit of good."

"You really are a cynical old woman."

"Tired," she corrected me, "very tired."

"But I will, you know, I will find what I'm looking for, even if it turns out not to be someone to love."

"Ah, a sacred calling," she murmured. "I knew it would come to that." She sealed her lips and entered a solitary, excluding silence. A moment later, she added: "But from here you must go on alone."

"This is where the old world and the new world part company? No more fireside chats? I've crossed a line too slippery even for you?"

"You'll come to visit. You are a deeply faithful person, where love is not concerned."

"You are saying good-bye?"

"You will visit, as I have said. But what you will bring to tell me I will no longer be able to understand."

26

Time comes down like snow. It swirls, drifts sideways, settles in, performs intricate patterns. But this behavior doesn't mean that time passes.

I could almost remember the way I had come apart, one particle at a time, when I had lost Sena. After that, I had let a cleavage fall through my life, making me someone who had never loved a woman. Names and facts stayed on, but they were worthless. The story of that love drifted apart, particle by particle; the past became a terrain I had mastered. I made it empty, cool, distant, unapproachable.

Where there is no time, nothing ever changes. If you shake yourself awake, if you come back to yourself, if you make yourself walk and breathe and stretch your legs, you might notice that the last grains of your life are now, in this very moment, falling.

Therefore, sooner or later, I would call Max, as I had before. I would call him, even if the call gave him satisfaction. I would go back when it turned out that I couldn't make it without him, couldn't make a living, would get into trouble. And so I waited,

I waited for it to happen, and it didn't happen. I woke up in the morning wondering if this was the day, the hour, the moment when the devastation would fall. It didn't fall. I kept glancing over my shoulder. Something was stalking me. There it was, making its way along a brittle, betraying woodland. I whirled around; I jumped back, startled. There was nothing. I was alone. Nothing was lying in wait for me. I was not being hunted.

I spent a lot of time with Aunt Edith during those weeks. In the first week we didn't talk much. She took care of her plants, fed the cats, watered the pots in her garden, fussed with the roses. I sat on the swing and brooded. The mortification struck hard. All those messages, my naïveté. Had she played my messages for Max? Had they laughed together about me? Was he triumphing over me? How easily he had taken possession of the woman I wanted. How easily she had given herself to him. Why him? Because he was mine? Because he was a version of me? Because she had planned it all along? Had I been the go-between, the passionate fool? I wouldn't believe it.

Late at night, when I woke up alone in my own house, the bleakness, the stark nowhere of my condition struck harder than mortification. Everything I had done had been done in her name. I had lived for her, become a boy for her, left Max, home, security, a known future for a woman who had probably already forgotten what we had said, what we had been, if so briefly, together. And the others? Alix Graham? The women with whom

I had gone dancing? They had become as insubstantial as water sprites. I felt that I had lived through an enchantment with them. I would sit straight up in bed to stare out at the fog-drenched view beyond my window, relieved to find a reflection of my inner state in the stark, dreary, drifting void. There was, I sensed, even there, something lilting, promised, almost grasped, sunburnt, beckoning. The few days at the conference had set up an enormous authority against the desolation that threatened me. One of these days, I would set out to find the women again and for that reason would survive the loss of Hadamar.

Maybe a boy isn't going to fall apart over a woman the way a woman does; maybe a boy isn't going to go to pieces the way I had gone to pieces over Sena. I thought Sena was the only woman in the world who would ever love me. A boy, the kind of boy I was now, knew it was his sexual destiny to love women. If he lost one, there would be others. When I loved Sena I believed there was only one woman I could love, there could never be another. When I couldn't keep that one there was no reason to go on living.

I had loved Sena as a woman.

During the second week Aunt Edith insisted that I spend the nights with her. She brought me a glass of milk when I lay in bed not sleeping, as if I were a small child, going through a restless period, who was dear and cherished and needed to be coddled.

In the third week I sank into an indifferent, stuporous state, refused to get up in the mornings, had to be prodded out into the garden, where I was assigned routine tasks I had trouble completing. In the fourth week I experienced episodes of sudden rage, slammed about through the garden, threw myself against the buckthorn tree, cursed out loud, wrote notes to Hadamar on scraps of paper, ripped them, threw them around the garden. Aunt Edith stood by with her hands on her hips, shaking her head. But I never cried. I was wildly, restlessly waiting for the whole thing to be over. It was the sort of thing you had to go through if you fell in love. The sort of thing I could endure and was now, because of what I had become, ready to master.

Then, one night, she sat me down for a talk.

"You give up easily, don't you," she said, dusting off a bench under the oak tree.

"You're trying to tell me to go back to Max? Impossible. Things have gone too far. I'm not the person I was, I couldn't go back, and why would he have me?"

"He expects you to be in a lot of trouble, he expects the phone to ring, he's waiting for you to be in need of rescue. Go ahead, try it out, pick up the phone. He'll be here before you can set down the receiver. But it's not Max I mean."

"Hadamar? I gave up Hadamar? Easily? What do you think I've been going through all these weeks? Easily? You can say that, easily?"

"Did you send Hadamar all those letters you wrote? Have you

spoken to her since you got back? Look at you. You've given up without a fight. You haven't stood up for your own desire, you haven't made your claim, you haven't uttered one word of anger. I expected more of you. I never thought you would give up so easily."

"It was you who said she would never make an unconventional choice. You said it yourself. Okay, I'm convinced."

"Too easily, that's what I say."

"Try to convince her she loves me more than she loves Max? Are you kidding?"

"Many people find you highly persuasive."

"But what good does it do me? Even if I know something about our relationship, Hadamar doesn't know, or has forgotten or arranged to forget. The minute I walk out the door she becomes someone else and I have to start all over again the next time we meet, winning her back, getting her to know me. If it was so difficult before, it would be impossible now, wouldn't it?"

"The reason to tell Hadamar what you feel about her has nothing to do with winning or losing. It has only to do with saying what you have to say. I know you, you will spend the rest of your life wondering what might have happened. It will tie you to Hadamar in a way you do not wish to be tied. You have no business binding yourself through Hadamar. You must speak to her, and you will speak to her," she said in a truly ominous tone. "Anything else would be cowardly. It would be an evasion."

"I guess you're tired of me. You could have told me, you know. I would have gone home sooner."

"*Qwatsch,* nonsense. Do what you have to do and be on your way. Did you think you were going to spend the rest of your life with an old woman?"

"I've liked it here. You've been very good to me . . ."

"Enough. I know what I've been," she said as she got up heavily. But her hand trailed lightly across my shoulders as she walked off.

27

I sent Hadamar the letters I had written from Santa Barbara. I thought I would probably have to wait a long time for a response, but a note arrived a few days later. She told me my writing was very impressive, that I was a great visionary and must bring my work out into the world. She would also be happy to see me whenever I cared to make a date with her.

I brought the note over to Aunt Edith.

"You hate her?" she laughed. "Good. Now you have a reason not to try further."

"Can you imagine what it will be like to try to arrange a date? I'll call, she'll call back, we'll set something up, something else will come up in the last minute, she'll be very apologetic, we'll arrange something else, something urgent will happen, she'll be charming and contrite, and it will go on forever."

"Did you forget the way to Hadamar's house? What happened to your key? Do you need a map to her private apartment?"

I knew Max was visiting our friend Lillian. Therefore I waited for Hadamar in the lovely room with French doors opening out into the garden. It seemed to have survived miraculously, unchanged through time, while I had become another person.

I recognized the way she opened the front door. I knew her step. I knew the minute I saw her I would fall in love all over again. I heard her going upstairs, and so I called out to her and waited for her to come find me.

She looked startled, ill-at-ease as she appeared in the doorway; she gestured vaguely as if to question my right to be there, laughed awkwardly, then took the situation in hand, so gracefully that I myself, if I had been observing her from a distance, would have been impressed.

"I knew I would find you here; I'm never wrong about such things where you're concerned," she said, as if I had come in answer to a summons and had no power of my own to disrupt her life.

I waited a long time before I said anything because I knew by now my silence could unsettle her. She went leisurely about the room, moving easily through those cool, severing moments, straightening a picture, adjusting the clock on the marble table.

"Well?" she said after a time, but without turning to face me. "I'm ready to listen."

There were thoughts I had prepared to say. I had written them on scraps of paper, in the margins of newspapers, on napkins, stuffed them into my pockets, planned to read them to her if I couldn't master the moment. I had jotted down a history of our relationship as it had played itself out over many generations. I was asking her to give up everything and go away with me. All evening, while I went from coffee shop to coffee shop, waiting for her to get home, I had written out every phase of grand and subtle and passionate feeling through which, I thought, we had passed together back through time.

I knew she would listen with her pointed silence, taking everything in, giving the impression you had never encountered so fine a listener, but as soon as the words died away she would have forgotten, they would mean nothing, they wouldn't have reached her.

This knowledge brought me an incredible detachment.

"You told me so many times you and Max were over," she said, finally, coming to stand in front of me as if we would face everything together. But she didn't sit down across from me on the square pillow where she had been sitting the day she told me the shortcut to her house, the day I ran all the way there without stopping.

She took a few steps toward me, suddenly eager to say more. "You have to admit I asked you as often as anyone could, no friend could have been more careful or more devoted. You assured me the relationship with Max was over. I can't count the number of times you insisted it was."

"Yes," I agreed, because I was already a long way from believing I had once counted so heavily on this woman. "You have been very devoted, very devoted."

"If you don't want him," she asked sharply, as if I had made her angry and she saw in anger her best way out, "why shouldn't I have him? You want to give him up but keep him in your back pocket? But I won't let you do that. I care too much for both of you to let you do that to him again."

I could see the blue veins in her temples. I noticed that her hands were shaking. I remembered my three gestures from months before, standing, moving resolutely, kneeling.

"You won't be able to do it," I said as I got to my feet. "Not even you can pull it off. There is no way in the world you can pretend all this has been about Max."

She took my hand. She raised it slowly and grandly in that way she had until it came to rest against her cheek.

"I don't want to lose you," she said, too loudly, into the complex emptiness of the beautiful room I thought I might have been seeing for the last time.

She was crying. They were the same slowly gathering tears she had wept over Stevens. They welled up in the corners of her eyes, then fell with their singular, slow dignity. I had seen her cry them so many times before. But this time she was crying over me.

"You won't lose me," I said gallantly, because I wanted to

believe she wouldn't have to. "All we have to do now is become friends."

She laughed at me the way she had from the beginning, from that day we ran into each other on the steps outside Aunt Edith's house, when Hadamar had seemed not to recognize me and pretended to believe the odd things I said were my eccentric humor.

I had told this woman more about my secret worlds than I had ever told anyone before, maybe because I had nothing to lose, because I had known all along she had never been able to take me seriously?

We have come to this, face to face in a room of departures. Hadamar is crying. Then it is so silent anything might still be done or said or take place. Our whole relationship is still here, still possible between us. We could wrap ourselves in a shawl and go sit in the garden. We could eat dried apricots and spend the rest of the night talking. I could accompany her at the piano, if she still sings. But I cannot make the single gesture of possession most men in my position would have made. I cannot act as she seems to expect me to act, putting an end to the intolerable tension of waiting that has always been there between us, always, from the first moment, as clear, ambiguous, inviting, and forbidding as it is now.

And yet I know exactly how to take her. I know what this gesture would be like, its unthinking, imperious quality, as if I were doing her a favor by wanting her. Take her hand, grasp her shoulder, take her by the hair, draw her close to me, put my arm around her waist, bend over her, smile down at her in the offhand assumption that she is honored, honored and has been paid tribute because I, the male, desire her. I have the raw sense of betrayal, the sharp hankering for revenge, the stiff belief that she owes me something. I have acquired, finally, the store of convictions that launch and empower an act of possession. The boy has risen to the full measure of his promise.

I experience my freedom to act as a giddy rush of intoxicated will, which charges the moment with its full erotic potential. I watch her eyes close, the lids trembling slightly. The acknowledgment that she has betrayed me, this confession she will never make, causes a perceptible tremor in her chin. Her entire body leans toward me, her head slightly tilted, her hands slowly opening. She wants this from me—an act in which all the evasions of our affair will be violently cast aside. I am capable of this; the boy is up and ready to go.

I watch her eyes open in a startled, outraged, unforgiving stare. It is a matter of seconds, of no time at all, in which there is just time to wonder if it's a question of shyness. No. This holding back, this refusal to act, this emphatic, virile hesitation, which I do not choose, or will, or even want, is my confession. I am ready for my freedom. If the boy puts his hands on her now he will fall victim to his own past. He has had his vision of abundance, a harvest waiting to be gathered in, a promised ripeness. Therefore, he is a ruthless master of disengagement.

We are moving to the door. It is one of those passages that will be repeated often in memory, examined, probed, scrutinized. But I will never believe that it might have been different.

Hadamar opens the door, hesitates, walks outside with me. Then, she abruptly turns back, shuts the door very carefully. She has gone over to the window in the music room and is watching me walk away. It's the sort of gesture she couldn't resist, and I, too, couldn't resist it if I turned to look at her. She has struck the pose in which she will be forever bidding me farewell. One hand drawing back the heavy curtain, the other hand pressed sadly against the windowpane—the woman for whom I could still ruin myself if I run back into the house to take her.

A blast of pure potential bolts on past me. I am not in pieces; I'm shaken but standing on my own feet. I walk off fast, without once thinking I should have turned back or still could or even want to, and to this day I cannot say that I regret it.

28

I used to think about Hadamar all the time, even after I went on into my life with women. I talked to Alix Graham about her and to Rain, another woman I came to know well. Alix and Rain thought passion of the kind I described—obsessive, possessive, exclusively focused on a single woman—was a holdover from my patriarchal upbringing, which I would transcend when I had lived long enough among women. They weren't much interested in my erotic musings about love as a transformational power; they laughed at me for being a romantic. I never spoke to either one of them about being a boy.

I used to wonder out loud what would have happened that night at the beach, when Hadamar was clinging to me because she couldn't come with me and couldn't let me go, if I had started to kiss her, right then and there. That night as we drove home, me driving her car, she put her head on my shoulder, but we never said a word until I walked her up the stairs to her front door, handed her back the keys, and didn't come in with her.

But if I had? What if I had? What if I had urged my advantage the way a born-boy would have done?

Hadamar said, "I have a feeling you are going very far away."

I said, "I'm taking a four-hour drive down the coast."

"Yes," she repeated, "a four-hour drive to an uncrossable threshold," and then hesitated, waiting, I thought, for me to act.

Rain and Alix had different responses to this moment. Rain thought I should have put an end to all the waiting and nonsense, taken her into the garden, and initiated her into matriarchal love. Rain was sure that was what Hadamar had expected from me. Alix felt I had sensitively read Hadamar's indecision and was right not to push the issue to a conclusion.

"We've all known a Hadamar," she said. "These women stand at the crossroads as if they are ready to go with you, pointing down the long road you will soon travel without them. Perhaps, without them, you might never have found your way to go beyond them, but they never do come with you. There are women like that—elusive, beckoning, the guardians of an ill-defined space between friendship and passion. They are there to break hearts. Then, those broken hearts will require a new life before they can be mended. You had lived most of your life as a man's woman. I suppose," she murmured with a contented smile, "your time had come to love women instead."

For a long time, even after I stopped mentioning Hadamar to anyone, I wondered how our lives might have turned out if I had behaved more like a born-boy, less like a crossover boy in my sailor shirt, with my short hair, my slim body, my passion for women, which never did learn to be tribal or collective or less possessive or any of the things I tried to learn from Alix and Rain and many others.

And so, yes, Edith proved to be right. Max and Hadamar would spend most of their time together for a while until he suggested they see each other less often because, he told her, he had so recently separated from me.

Hadamar was offended; she withdrew from him and they never saw each other again, although we all lived in the same city for a long time.

A few years later she married an art collector from Safed, a man who had lots of money and many affairs, but she came back home to Berkeley when she left him. Max never heard from her again. I myself received a card written in a fine, spindly hand, a few weeks after she got back, making it clear I could come to see her but without actually inviting me. I thought about going but was perhaps afraid then that if we ever met up, in this life or any other, the same love and risk and betrayal would happen again.

Perhaps in our last meeting, when Hadamar didn't refuse and I didn't act, I was holding out for our mutual surrender. I trusted to nothing that was moved along by the wandering eros of the moment, to be denied or regretted the next morning.

The boy, as I have always said, is a transitional figure. When he arrives at the supreme moment of his fulfillment—the capacity to act, the freedom to take, the license to choose his desire—he has just bumped up against his own future. If he is the sort of boy who is constantly moving forward, his future will exercise a more profound and compelling erotic power than any singular act of possession. Why should he accept one woman when he can have them all? Why should he put up with repetition when something new is about to take place? As a boy, he senses in the inexorable thrust of his own development the promise of power, liberation, license, opportunity. Things can only get better. He won't settle for less than everything he might have.

What will happen to him then? Will he go on being a boy forever? Will he turn into a man of sensibility or even into a woman? Perhaps there is a new kind of woman that comes to exist only by passing through the transitional phase of a boy.

As for me, I always knew there was a great love in store for me. If it wasn't Hadamar, it would be someone else. I only had to set out looking, and keep on looking, and never stop until the right love came along. If I had cunning and persistence and sufficient passion to break with the present in the name of the future, sooner or later, I knew, I would find the one to whom this story could be told.